Just Joey

A LEGEND IN HIS OWN ZOOMIES

ALISON J MOORE

Just Joey

A legend in his own zoomies

Enquiries; author.amoore@gmail.com

Cover design and illustrations, by Alison J Moore©

The names of some characters *may* have been changed to preserve anonymity.

www.alisonjmoore.com

Preface

The following story is based on actual events and retold with the words of both owner and dog.

Midlife crisis?

Maybe, but I was past midlife: whenever that is!

What I did know was that my life was devoid of love and affection: I had been single too long.

After much thought and consideration, I felt the time was right to have a dog in my life again and decided to search for a rescue dog, but he found me.

Little did I realise how it was going to affect my life.

Chapter One

There were people everywhere.

All above me: ignoring me.

They were around Dad's bed.

He was being taken, not roughly, and he wasn't protesting. But he couldn't.

I needed to stop them.

But I was too small.

I was picked up; I kicked, and I bit.

I quietened as the other people left.

I looked at the bed. There was a dent where he had been. It was a warm spot I sometimes curled into, smelling his scent, relaxing, and falling asleep until I was called for breakfast. I tried to scramble free to get to that spot, to feel warm and safe, but I was held close and taken from the room.

I cried.

I shivered and curled up tighter: it was minus two

degrees, and I was not in my comfy bed. I wasn't even in my house.

Or with my family.

I was in a cell.

Concrete walls and floors stank of disinfectant, and there was a warm breeze from somewhere.

It was dark. I heard others breathing, but no one was there with me. I curled up on my bedding; at least, this was mine. It smelled of Dad, and it helped me relax.

I heard other dogs barking and crying; where was I?

Footsteps came along the passageway, and I blinked as the winter sun came through the bars on the windows. The latch was lifted on my cell. I edged back into the corner, frightened of what was to come. Two bowls were placed before me. My nose twitched: biscuits and water. The rosy-cheeked girl who had brought them in ruffled my fur, smiled and left; onto the next. I edged my way towards the bowls, sniffing the air. It smelled good, and I took a small mouthful. I was not hungry, and I felt sad more than anything. But I ate a little before curling back into the corner of my bed; I tucked my nose under my leg and cried quietly.

The daily routine was the same. The lovely girls came in and fed me; they always smiled, cuddled me, and spoke to me in comforting tones. I didn't understand what they were saying, but they were kind.

The girls were friendly, but I didn't like being there and missed my dad. Where was he? The rosy-cheeked girl clipped a lead on me, walked me down the corridor past other cells, and led me into the grassy paddock. My nose twitched, and my tail gave a slight wag. I could smell other dogs, horses, and, my nose twitched again, cats! I wandered around, sniffing here and there and marking my territory.

There was an old boy in the corner, an Alsatian. His fur was dull and in clumps; he was very old indeed. He limped from stiffness in his back legs when he got up to walk. He was almost blind, so he sensed his way around the paddock, but Rosy Cheeks told me he had been there so long that he rarely bumped into anything. He moved from corner to corner, changing the blurred view from sheep to cars in the car park. This was his home, and he would spend his last days here. We sniffed each other with respect, and I left him alone.

Rosy Cheeks called my name, and I glanced at her. She had a lead in her hand, but I continued to sniff around. She called me again, leant forward and patted her knees. I only responded to Dad, so I ignored her. She walked over, gently lowered the loop over my head, slid up the toggle, ruffled my head, and gave me a gentle tug on the lead. Walkies.

We were out in the countryside; I was not used to all the smells. I came from a town that was busy with cars and people. Here, it smelled different; I especially liked the horse poo and how it clung to my long coat; for some reason, I found that quite comforting. We trudged around the muddy field, my little paws picking their way in the ruts whilst Rosy Cheeks squelched in the mud, sometimes giggling as she got stuck and had to tug her welly out. She talked to me all the time and even sang. I pretended not to take any notice; I just sniffed, scratched at the earth and peed.

When we returned to the cells, she sprayed water on my legs, dried me, and brushed my coat. I didn't like being brushed, but I let her do it. The less fuss I made, the sooner I could go home.

Chapter Two

It was a lovely winter weekend. Crisp and bright. I was sitting in the conservatory working on a pet portrait. When I am drawing, I get locked into the subject, and this one was a beauty. A couple of 'Chugs', Chihuahua and Pug cross puppies. These two little boys were curled up together on a blanket. Their beautiful golden colouring merged them. As I couldn't see any open eyes as they were asleep, I had to focus on the nose to discern which way around they were! It was complex and absorbing. Then the phone rang.

"Blooming phone when I'm trying to draw." I looked at the caller, Jayne, my neighbour. I sighed, put my fistful of pencils down and grabbed the phone.

"Hi, Hun. Are you still interested in a dog?"

"Er, yes, of course. Why?"

"Think we've found you one. Come to the pub, and we'll take you to see him."

The phone went dead. I did that daft thing; I looked

at the phone and then down at myself: pyjama bottoms and a sweatshirt. Well, it was Sunday, but now I had better get dressed. The drawing of the Chugs could wait until later.

On the 10-minute drive, I wondered what sort of dog they had found. Big or small, old or a puppy. Where had it come from, and why? I'd soon find out. I parked in the pub car park, took a deep breath, and walked in through the door. As I walked through the bar, Jayne's three Border Terriers caught sight of me and yapped excitedly. Carl, Jayne's husband, thrust a glass of wine into my hand, and a stool was vacated for me to sit down. Three wet noses wanted my attention before anything else. I scratched their heads before asking Jayne about the dog.

"Oh, it's so sweet. It's a Cocker Spaniel crossed with a Sheltie, ever so friendly, and it's up at the kennels."

"Long-haired?"

Jayne put her hand on my arm. "I know you didn't want long-haired, but wait until you see him; he's gorgeous." I raised an eyebrow; she knew I was a tough nut to crack but a softie when it came to dogs. She continued, "He's ten years old, and his owner died suddenly. The son had no time for a dog, so he dropped him into the kennels hoping to find a home rather than take him to a rescue centre."

I sipped on my drink and wondered what the heck I was doing. I knew having a dog again would completely change my life; I'd been weighing the pros and cons for years. I would be responsible for a living, breathing, demanding dog, and I still wasn't sure I was ready for that again. But I had been single for eight years, and there was a gaping hole in my life. My home was devoid of life and love. No man had yet come into my life for more than a blink of an eye, and I was sadly very lonely even though I went out with many friends for meals and the theatre. With a dog around, I would have a purpose to my days other than running my business, but was I too set in my ways? There was only one way to find out.

We left the pub for the kennels, and more Border Terriers ran in and out of my legs. A white cat scowled as it sauntered past me and headed for the warmth of my car bonnet, whether I liked it or not. In a fenced-off muddy paddock, I saw an ancient Alsatian with glazed eyes; he was blind, and his nose twitched as he scented the air. I put my hand on the fence, and he nuzzled it. A rosy-cheeked girl came from the kennels with what looked like a miniature border collie and headed towards us.

"This is Joey."

I knelt to say hello; he seemed disinterested. His coat was very long, almost touching the floor. He sniffed at me, and I reached out to fuss him. He looked a little tubby, but my hand sank into a very thick coat of fur: he was a tiny chap underneath it all, standing about 12" high to his shoulder. She gave me the lead, and we went off for a little walk around the field. We plodded in mutual silence; Joey never looked up once. I cut across the field and headed across the tractor tracks to the opposite side. Joey still carefully placed his feet in the tracks but did not bother if a puddle was in the way; he just plodded straight through it.

He seemed such a sad little chap; how could I not give him a home?

A week later, I returned. Joey was in the paddock, sitting in the opposite corner to the Alsatian. I got out of the car, and he jumped up the fence. Was he pleased to see me? I'm sure I saw a slight wag of the tail.

I had a new collar and lead for him as this little boy was coming home with me.

Chapter Three

I heard a car; I wondered who was coming today. Was it Dad?

I looked across from the paddock; it was That Lady again, laughing with the big man who locked us up at night. She had something in her hand. I put my paws up the fence for a closer look; it was a new red collar and lead.

Rosy Cheeks came into the paddock and called me. That Lady had given her the collar and lead: they were for me! It had been a long time since I had a new collar, and this one was bright red. Rosy Cheeks led me towards her and said goodbye with a big hug, and then That Lady picked me up and fussed me. I liked that because she was warm, soft, and scratched behind my ears. She then put me on the seat in her car. She shook hands with the big man and got in the car, and we started moving. I barked.

I barked at the trees as we passed.

I barked at the horses.

I barked, and I barked.

Where were we going?

I was scared and tried to get onto her lap, but she pushed me back, muttering something about driving. We stopped, but I carried on barking. She opened the door and encouraged me out. Grass, bushes, pee.

In through a door. Carpet under my feet. I hadn't felt a carpet for weeks, so I sniffed it. She took my lead off and talked to me as I sniffed the sofa and the table. I didn't know what she was saying, but she was smiling. I was rooted to the spot, listening: was Dad here? She put a water bowl down, and I drank as she opened another door. The smell of fresh air flooded in, and it was the fresh air I was used to, including coal smoke, cars, and people. Then I smelled something else and edged towards the door. My nose rose, and my heart beat faster...cats!

I hesitated. I didn't want to go into a cold cell again. Was it a trap? Should I go out? She walked ahead of me, and I slowly followed. I sniffed around not far from the door, peed, and then ran back inside. She laughed. I waited until the door was shut before I drank again. I didn't know where I was or what was happening, but I felt okay here. Maybe Dad was turning up later.

I jumped onto the chair, felt the fluffy cushion under my feet, and curled up to wait.

Chapter Four

I sat and watched him as he slept. He had hardly moved since we had come home. I assumed he was unsettled, so I didn't worry about it, but I found it hard to watch TV and relax. He was curled in such a tight ball on the chair that you couldn't see where he started or ended, just a bundle of long fur, asleep but tense; the poor thing. He had been through a lot the last few weeks and must be confused.

He was such a pretty boy. He looked like a miniature black-and-white border collie with little spots on his muzzle and fluffy paws. I immediately forgot my misgivings about having a long-coated dog.

I carried on with my everyday chores around the house like he wasn't there; he watched every move but stayed curled up tight. I sat down with my dinner on a tray; he raised his head, stretched, sniffed the air, and then curled back up again. A dog not interested in human food? There was a first.

He watched as I put on my shoes and picked up his lead; he started to move, then stopped. I had no idea what he was thinking, but I knew he needed to stretch his legs. I clipped the lead on and led him around the block, allowing him to sniff and pee. He wasn't bothered by the traffic whizzing past or the noise. He was spending time taking in the new aromas and making his mark.

Back home, I put his dinner down. I didn't know what food he was used to, so I offered him a mix of tinned meat and biscuits. He half-heartedly ate some of the meat before returning to the chair and curling up. All I could see were his eyes peering at me. Before long, he was sound asleep; I hoped he felt safe.

He started to snore, stretched his legs and twitched; was he chasing something? Then, quiet for a short while, his paws twitched again, and he cried. Cries as I'd never heard from a dog, like a kitten mewing for its mother. His eyelids flickered; what dream was the poor boy having? I didn't know whether to wake him or let him be. The crying and twitching continued, and I also felt tears in my eyes. I gently called his name. Slowly, the cries died, and the twitches stopped. He lifted his head as he opened his eyes. He blinked, then sat bolt upright, looking around fearfully as he woke from a deep sleep: he didn't know where he was. I gently called his name again, and I gave him space to settle before going to him and gathering him up for a cuddle.

Chapter Five

It had gone dark. I was stiff after being curled up so tightly. I wasn't scared, but I was nervous and sad. I wondered where she had gone as she wasn't on the sofa. It was very quiet. All I could hear was the ticking of the clock. I stayed on the chair until I was sure she wasn't returning. Inquisitively, I decided to explore and find her. I snuffled around the kitchen and found a floor raisin, a stray bit of chicken that had dropped to the floor when she had served her dinner earlier. Into the conservatory, I put my paws up to the window ledge, but it was so dark that I could only see my reflection in the pale light from a side lamp. I jumped up on the conservatory chair. It rocked a little, so I quickly got back down again. What should I do next?

I crept upstairs and went through the first door on the left. There was a bed and some boxes. I sniffed. No, she wasn't in here. The next room smelt clean and fresh with a scent that made my nose twitch; it was the bathroom. With only one more door to enter, I knew it was where she would be; I could smell her. I sniffed around the bed and quietly jumped onto the bottom corner; I doubted she knew I was there. A soft bed, warm and cosy, like I shared with Dad; it just smelled different: more girly. A hand reached down: would I be thrown off the bed? Her hand ruffled my fur; phew, it was okay to be here. I stretched and made my way up the quilt to her end and looked at her. She looked normal enough and had let me stay on her bed. It was much better than those cold cells. Her hand reached out towards me again. She was doing that thing with my ears again; it was heavenly. I relaxed and lay beside her, feeling her warmth through the quilt. She continued to stroke me as I went to sleep.

OMG, I need to pee! I jumped off the bed. Where do I go? Where do I go? Stairs: downstairs, and there must be a door; which door? OMG, I need to pee!

OPEN THE DOOR!

Panic, I didn't know where to go. In the cell, there was just the space I was in unless we were in the yard. I heard her come running down the stairs. She saw the panic in my eyes as I stood by the front door, then called me to another door. Without thought, I dived down the steps, sniffed the fresh air, and relaxed. Oh, that feeling when...pure ecstasy and I scuffed the grass in delight. She stood there looking at me; I looked back indifferently and wanted another pee. I decided to explore the garden.

We had a garden at Dad's, but it was much nicer. Dad cut the grass and stuff, and there were lots of flowers that smelled sweet that I got shooed off if I walked on. Then there were flutterby things that I watched, but they were too high to catch. There were black and yellow buzzing things, zigzagging around from one flower to the next. I didn't try to catch those; I knew from experience that they hurt. I managed to get one once, and after it stopped buzzing in my mouth, it stuck something into me that made my nose scrunch up and my tongue scrape against my teeth. No, those little beggars could be left alone. Spicy sky-raisins were the enemy.

This garden was far from as nice, but it was exciting. Brambly hedges and droopy trees that I could swish the branches of as I walked under, and some tiny gaps under the fence. I poked my nose in and discovered another nose. "Yap, yap", I stepped back in shock; that wasn't me; who was it? I poked my nose in again, and the same little black nose was there; he moved, and another took his place. "Yap, yap". I wagged my tail and tried to squeeze my head through to see the wet black noses again, but I felt a pair of hands around my middle; it was her. She picked me up and talked to someone on the other side of the fence. I looked down to see that the gap was now black. It had been blocked off. Bugger.

Lead on, we headed out the door, and the lights of the car flashed as she unlocked it. Oh no, was she taking me back to the cells? Please don't take me back to the cells. I trusted you! I barked, please, no, don't do it! I barked, and I barked. I tried to put my paw on her shoulder but couldn't reach it as I was in a harness, so I continued to bark.

We were in the car for a long time before we stopped. It wasn't the cells, but it was another building. Where were we now? She was talking to me; she said it was somewhere called work.

She unlocked the door, unset the alarm and shut the door before unclipping my lead. There were lots of weird smells in this place. I had not encountered smells of machinery, grease and printing ink. She walked past me as I explored the nooks and crannies while she went into the kitchen. Food and water were put down for me, and as I entered her office, there was a big soft bed on the floor. Was there another dog? I sniffed it warily. No, it was brand new; it must be for me. I nibbled at my food. I still wasn't really hungry, and I wouldn't say I liked this stuff much either, but once I'd had a little, I went and lay on the bed, scratching it all into place and shut my eyes. I was exhausted.

She was calling me again. I struggled to open my eyes. I just wanted to sleep and feared I was in the cells again every time I woke up. She dangled the lead in front of me. My tail thumped on the bed, and I looked at it; I didn't say you could wag, behave! A new place and a new walk. This outside smelled different: lots of oil and metal, wood and fumes from chimneys belching smoke. This place was strange. People were walking to and fro, shouting and waving at each other. Lorries and trucks were coming and going. Whilst I was trying to absorb this, something caught my eye. I froze; what was that I could see? I looked around, and then I saw it again: fox.

There was a bloody fox. And it was daylight.

This is my walk down here now, mate; what are you doing? Quit scavenging on my patch. Go on, get lost.

The little bugger. He was strolling across the yard like he owned it. He hadn't seen me; he hadn't even scented me.

This scrag-end of a town fox in its brindle coat wasn't even noticing the workers on their cigarette break. I pulled towards him, but she wasn't having it. Damn. I wanted that fox.

I tugged at the lead to follow his scent down the track, weaving this way and that. She wasn't amused as I was getting under her feet. Where had he come from?

Where was he going?

All the way around the block, I was thinking of that fox. I'd lost his scent. Damn.

Chapter Six

"JOEY!"

The second I had slackened the lead after we returned to the work unit, the little beggar had slipped his head out, turned tail, and ran. Fear and panic ran through my bones, and I wanted to be sick. I left the door open with my keys in the lock and ran after him. Was he going to turn to the left or the right? Right was the way we had come, and left was to the main road. Please, Joey, turn right; I didn't want to hear the squeal of brakes.

Right. He turned right. I stopped running and tried to calm myself. Deep breaths: he was after that fox. I caught sight of his black tail with the white tip as he paused for a pee. He was barely 20 paces ahead of me. I called him, trying to keep the panic from my voice, but he was off again, nose to the ground following the scent of the fox.

Don't panic; he would sense it, I told myself.

Don't shout; he would think he had done wrong and run faster and further.

What was I doing putting myself through the possibility of losing him within 24 hours of having him?

"JOOEEEEEEEEY."

I had lost sight of him.

Yeah, yeah, I can hear you, but I needed to see.

FOX. FOX. FOX. FOX. Come on, foxy. Where did you go? Nose down to the ground, I was off!

"JOEY!"

I took no notice; I was okay and knew what I was doing.

I.

Want.

That.

Fox.

She was coming. I sidestepped into the gates. At least she wasn't running after me.

I heard the gates close. But she couldn't see me. She was still calling, but the scent was gone.

"Come on, boy, let's go home and get some treats." I looked left and right, and I couldn't see him. But I saw the fox; it appeared on my right from around the back of a factory. We looked at each other, separated by a chain-link fence. He blinked, turned tail, and slunk off with an abandoned piece of Kentucky Fried Chicken.

I called again. The fox was inside a gated area, so I assumed Joey had gone there too. I pulled both gates shut. Yes, there was enough gap underneath for him to get under, but I hoped it would have delayed him and slowed him down if he tried to run past me. My heart was settling back to normal as I scanned the open space. Thankfully, no wagons or forklift trucks were moving around; otherwise, my panic could have reached new levels.

"JOEY!"

I saw a flash of white go past a skip at the bottom of the yard. I had no idea if there was an exit that way but hoped not; I waited. Joey came around the bottom unit, nose down to the ground again, then up in the air. He stopped when he saw me and defiantly cocked his leg up a drain pipe. A bunch of guys on a cigarette break were watching him, too. Thankfully, they hadn't seen me and didn't try to scare Joey off. He was coming towards me at a leisurely pace. I loosened the loop of the lead and crouched down.

The fox was gone. Damn.

Another day, I'd get him.

I strolled along the units as if it was a normal thing to do. I knew I was going to get a roasting. But she wasn't shouting; why not?

We walked back to work past neighbouring units. All were busy with their own lives, unaware of the drama that had just occurred in mine. I would have nightmares that night, that's for sure.

When I got back to my bed, I had dreams of that scraggy runt of a fox; I chased it around the yard, in and out of units, telling it to get off my land, off my dog walk. What spoils on that patch are mine, Mr. Fox, so don't return.

Tomorrow, I will try to get him again.

Tomorrow, I must be careful not to let Joey get the upper hand. Very, very careful!

Chapter Seven

It was nearly the end of my second week with Shemom, and it was okay. But oh no, we were in the car again. Where were we going today? I couldn't help but feel scared every time we got in the car. I wasn't used to cars and was still afraid of returning to the cells. I hated it there; it was just horrid. Surely, after that lovely lie-in, we weren't going to work again? I whined straight into Shemom's ear.

But we had stopped already after only driving a short distance down the road. We left the car and walked past a place smelling of sausages and bacon cooking; I wanted to go in there. Then there was a place where I could smell many dogs and cats; Shemom said it was the V E T. Then, I could hear high-pitched squawks from birds. I heard Aunty Laura being mentioned, and the noise was getting louder. Aunty Laura has a shop, and a bell rang as Shemom pushed the door. Much noise was coming from within: squawks, squeaks, squeals, a jingle of bells and voices. All sorts of voices. And smells.

Oh, what smells! My nose twitched in delight. I raised my nose and sniffed. I could scent...I twitched again; straw, that was it; straw. A high-pitched squawk made me wince as a beady eye watched me enter from behind a set of bars. I looked up at the grey parrot, who was staring and squawking at me. I didn't want that beak anywhere near me, thank you! Nose down, I followed the scent of the straw; I ignored Shemom and all the other humans. I bumped noses with a bit of wood, then a mesh and, oh, hello, a pink twitchy nose, whiskers, and fluffy fur. But not a dog, not like me, no. His nose twitched again; oops, no, he is a she. A tiny paw quickly fired towards me, and she bopped me on the nose through the mesh for being so nosy.

Humph. I moon-walked backwards, offended by her reaction. But I was also excited by it; what was that creature? Dogs I knew, cats I knew, I think I grew up with them, but I couldn't remember. Foxes, I knew, they smelled awful, and they sprayed on my garden. My garden, how dared they? But what was this fluffy thing that challenged me? I looked up at Shemom, who was taking no notice as she was chatting, so I slid forward, paratrooper-style, on my belly. Low down, I was sure she couldn't see me, so the advantage was mine. I reached the wood and raised my nose to the mesh... boff! She got me again. I skittered backwards, quivered in excitement and barked. Then I heard a little squeak like two balloons rubbing together. My head snapped to the right, and the next bit of mesh...a russet and white face with a twitchy nose...who was this little chap? Distracted now, I commando-crawled again; I approached the mesh. Boff! It was another boffy thing, but it missed me, hah! I was wise to your boffy mate over there; you're not going to get me again!

There were many boffy things at ground level, and I looked at them all: long-eared fluffy ones, brown ones, white ones with cute long lashes, baby ones, adult ones, and even a pair in a cage that was...oh... I think they were...I turned away.

Aunty Laura was talking to Shemom, and I could smell something on this bag. I sniffed...ooh straw, I raised my leg and peed. This place was heaven; I wanted a boffy thing to play with, some straw to sniff, and that bag I had peed up. Aunty Laura bent down to cuddle me. She was nice. She was smiley and smelt of dogs and boffy things. She needed to have kisses, and I gave her lots. She wasn't mad at me even when she realised that I had peed up her straw. She just mopped it up and gave me a treat.

We left Aunty Laura's loaded with goodies: lots of chewy treats, squeaky toys and a fluffy bunny that looked just like the boffy things in the cages. I liked it there. Shemom, can we go again? I was looking forward to my treats when I got home.

We returned home, and as we went into the lounge, Shemom wrinkled her nose,

"What's that smell?"

I admit it was a very unpleasant smell, and I knew what it was, but I kept quiet. I felt I might be in the dog house or, worse still, be sent back to the cell. I quickly jumped up onto the chair and pretended to sleep. I knew nothing, honest.

Shemom had been sitting with her feet up and trying to

identify the smell for days but couldn't work out what it was or where it was coming from. She'd checked the fridge and wiped it out with disinfectant. It wasn't that. She'd emptied the outside bin and disinfected that, too. She shut the back windows in case it was drifting in from somewhere, but every time we came into the house, she could smell it. Then, just as we were off to bed, she dropped to the floor, sniffing like a bloodhound. Uh oh, my number was up as she neared the far end of the sofa.

"Joey!"

I cringed; she'd found it. I couldn't look and hid behind the chair. She was wiping her hand on the edge of the sofa and the carpet; her hand was wet. She sniffed it, and her nose wrinkled. I didn't think puppy eyes would work at this point. Copious amounts of kitchen towel flowed from her hands like a white bouquet as she dropped it on the spot where I had peed. She mumbled something again, but I kept well away.

All she did was look at me with those eyes-not, the lovey-dovey, you are my best boy, eyes, but the slightly kooky Hell-raiser ones.

I slept on the landing most of the night before I crept onto the bed and made myself so tiny in the corner that she would overlook that I was there. In the morning, the smell was still there, so Shemom consulted the oracle of Google before rinsing with water and applying a nose-wrinkling concoction of vinegar and water before more paper towels were weighed down with a brick. Success, no smell. I kept myself out of the way and made myself busy in the conserva-

tory, fly catching. I knew I'd impress her with this. Cats brought mice, I caught flies, simple.

Now I knew that the end of the sofa wasn't for peeing up; I would be good and not do it there again. Apart from the fact it now stank of vinegar, which was not very appealing.

One of the other battles I had with Joey was his food. He was a picky eater. He ate and drank delicately and only ate as much as he wanted, which was very little with what I was feeding him. I tried all the dog food brands in my local supermarket, but he turned his nose up at them. As for biscuits, they were left behind in the bowl or on the surrounding floor. He would pick the biscuits up, suck the meat off and then spit the biscuit out. Often walking a few paces into the lounge and depositing them there. I think he was trying to make a point! Unfortunately, if I was walking around barefoot, I either ended up with a soft biscuit squished between my toes or trod on a dry one that had me doing the, stepped on a Lego brick, dance.

Finding a dog food he liked cost me a small fortune in different brands. Eventually, we got around to trying Pal. That seemed to hit the spot. Half a tin of that, and he was happy, as long as it didn't entail having to eat the biscuits unless he wanted to. But at least he was eating, so I was pleased. The unopened tins of everything else went into the dog rescue charity bins at the supermarket. At least some other dog would be grateful for all the money I had spent on tinned dog food.

Chapter Eight

It was the following night when IT happened. I raised an eyebrow as I heard her call my name and heard my lead rattle. WALKIES! Excitement and turning in circles and whoops and woofs of delight; WALKIES! Where are we going? It was evening, and we were getting in the car. Oh no, had I blown it this time? Was I being returned to the cell? Now I was scared. I barked, and I yelped, NOOO!

A short drive later, Shemom parked the car in line with several others. I sniffed the air. We were not at the park, but I could smell other dogs. I could see little dogs, big dogs, puppy dogs and old dogs. We followed a cute little Pomeranian through some doors, and then I was nose to chest with a big black Great Dane. He just sat there, cool as a cucumber, looking down at me. I looked away and saw more dogs. The other shemoms were smiley and bent down to give me a fuss. This wasn't a cell. It was a happy place, and I liked these shemoms and dads, but it was a strange room. The blue plastic sheeting spread across the floor crinkled as we walked.

I'd never adopted an older dog before and didn't realise they needed as much attention, if not more, than puppies. With a puppy, you knew you had to train them to pee in the right place, sleep on their bed, walk on a lead, and generally behave. I thought that if I adopted an older dog, it would have all these qualities in place and more. A happy, well-trained dog that would settle in quickly with love and attention and quickly bring a rewarding relationship. I was wrong. Joey and I were struggling to bond, and he was driving me bonkers with his barking in the car, sometimes to the point of tears.

Had I made a colossal mistake, or was I doing something wrong? Not one to give in, I called a local training club, spoke to Peter, and explained the situation. After saying that he may just be that kind of dog that barks, he said he was happy for me to come to puppy training lessons, hoping to improve our relationship and build a bond. He invited us to watch the last session, which was currently running, to see how things worked. I was full of nerves. Joey tended to bark at other dogs, so I was apprehensive about how he would behave in a room full of them. The barking in the car on the short journey didn't help my nerves. I sat in the car park for a few minutes as various fluff balls emerged from vehicles. Some were proud and cocky; others dragged their owners to the nearest blade of grass; others were carried in a protective embrace like they were a baby.

Joey would look odd at ten years old amongst all these

yappy little youngsters. Time was ticking away, and we needed to enter or miss seeing the class. With his lead firmly in place, we entered the hall. Joey's eyes were everywhere, and then his head went back, and he began to bark and then bark some more. All eyes turned toward us, and I wanted the ground to open up and swallow me whole.

A Cockerpoo looked at us with disgust and went back to licking his paw, a blue Staffordshire Bull Terrier wagged and panted in our direction, and then the worst thing that could have happened happened: a Yorkshire Terrier joined in the barking, closely followed by an Alsatian. They sounded like a poorly tuned orchestra. Two ladies who sat behind a table with two Shelties underneath raised their heads and looked in my direction. No shush and quiet from me made any difference. I went a pale pink in the face before graduating to a burning crimson.

Thankfully, a kind soul came over with some treats. Joey gratefully relieved her of them before I approached the ladies table to show Joey's inoculation certificates and sign in. Joey had gone quiet and was not the slightest bit interested in the two Shelties. Can dogs connect with the breeds they are related to?

We moved to the right and up the steps onto the stage. As I sat on a chair, Joey slunk between my legs to hide: the bravado bark had ceased, and I sensed he was a little scared. Then his nose popped out and twitched. He hadn't noticed the little Pomeranian sitting on her owner's lap at the other end of the row of chairs, but his nose had picked up that she was close by. He eased out from under me and stuck his nose in the air. A tentative paw went in her direction, then another. I kept a tight rein on his lead as I could see she was timid, but after a few steps, Joey did something unusual for him; he sat and stared at her. There was a little twitch from the end of his tail, and as she began to whine, he dropped his head to one side, stared some more, and then wined back at her. I called him back towards me, and he reluctantly turned and padded back.

I saw two Spaniels lazing by some chairs as I was led up a few steps onto a stage. We were above everyone, and I could see all the other dogs. Hello, the cute little Pomeranian was sitting next to me, too. But what was going on below us? They were all walking in circles, and I sniffed the air; they were being given bacon!

The man with the black Great Dane was in the middle of the blue plastic, and he introduced himself as Peter. His deep voice sounded like my dad, but he wasn't my dad. Maybe I was here to find Dad? I looked around. Many people and dogs stood in a circle around Peter and the Great Dane. Some dogs sat quietly by their owners; others were sniffing at the owner's pockets. That's where treats were kept. I knew that, as I remember being trained when I was little, Dad would give me a treat when I was good. I liked treats, but now that I was older, I wanted soft treats, not biscuit ones. I didn't like biscuits with my dinner. They were horrid. I would snuffle in my bowl, nose all the biscuits out, and eat the meat. But the meat Shemom gave me was awful and different from what I was used to, so I only ate some of my dinners. Why couldn't she give me what I was used to? I wondered if Shemom had got treats in her pocket. The only way I could find out was by jumping on her lap, and as she was watching the other dogs, I did just that. She was surprised, but I took no notice and snuffled in her jacket pocket to find treats.

There were no treats, just a tissue, so I took that instead. I jumped down to see a golden Cocker Spaniel with his paws on the stage, and he was looking at me. He was friendly, and I strained on my lead to speak to him. His tail was wagging, so I wagged mine. Then a lady leant over, and she had treats! They were lovely treats; they tasted like sausage!

The big man was speaking again, and as he did so, I saw a Jack Russell go to the water bowl, but he did not drink. He sniffed at the wall behind it and then cocked his leg up to pee! One of the Sheltie ladies came out with a mop and bucket, and the Jack Russell was getting told off. His mom told him it was his second time in puppy training and that he should know better by now. He looked at her, yapped, and wagged his tail. His poor mom was mortified. But that's what we dogs do; we like a smell and pee on it.

The puppies were now walking around the room. Sometimes, they sat, then they would lie down, and then they would get a treat. I wanted to walk on the blue plastic thing to get treats!

It was nice to watch how the class worked, and Joey's good behaviour would certainly do us good when we joined the new class the following week. I waited until most of the dogs had gone before I led Joey off the stage and said my goodbyes before heading to the car to go home. Then Joey started to bark again. Would he ever be quiet?

Chapter Nine

We were off to the place called work again, but I was still trying to figure out where we were going every time we got into the car. I was so scared of returning to the cell that I barked in fear. Also, I had only been in a car occasionally. My Dad and I walked everywhere, so these car things were strange. I wouldn't say I liked the other cars swishing past, but I couldn't understand why Shemom didn't fuss me when I only wanted to sit on her lap and feel safe.

When we arrived, I ate a little breakfast and then slept on my bed. I liked my new bed; it was soft, comfy, and safe. Shemom was also working on the computer, doing design stuff, she called it. She talked to me a lot, but I pretended not to notice. I didn't want to like Shemom as much as I loved Dad.

I was woken by a man's voice at the unit's door. I wondered who this was; he had a funny accent. I got up and looked up at the thing called a counter. I had to wait for people to come to me as I was only small. This face with glasses on peered over the counter with a big smile, and he was talking to me! I wagged my tail, and he brought his hand down to me so that I could sniff it. I wrinkled my nose; it smelled of grease and oil, but I still let him scratch the top of my head. Shemom picked me up, and the man came around the counter. I was face to face with him now, and he was still smiling.

He leant towards me, and I could see a big hair sprouting in the middle of his nose; I wondered if I could get it. I sniffed at his face, and he let me sniff as much as I liked. Then I gave his nose a big lick. He laughed, so I gave him another, then another. He said they were kisses, but I wanted to tell him no; it was the fact I wanted the hair on his nose. He said I was beautiful and would be good for Shemom, whatever that meant, and then he put something on the counter. I sniffed. Ugh, it was chocolate. Silver foil and red paper: I think it said KitKat. It was Shemom's treat from Micky Muppet. He was a lovely man.

We went back to the office, and Shemom made a cup of tea, which she drank while talking on the phone. The phone was noisy and kept waking me up. At lunchtime, I was woken by a lady's voice as she came in the door. She didn't wait for me to reach the counter; she came into the office and bent down to me straight away. She said her name was Paula and that she loved me. She smelt divine, and I gave her a lick; she tasted nice too! She was very smiley and happy and had no hairs on her nose, but I licked it anyway. She let me carry on licking, and she, too, called it kisses. I was wagging my tail as I liked licking, no, kissing, people's faces. If you got near their mouth, you could taste what they had had for dinner!

Then this lady, Paula, picked up my lead, took some treats, and we were off for a walk! I heard Shemom telling her to watch out for the fox. Bugger, I was hoping to catch him this time, but no chance now that Paula was alerted to his presence.

We had a lovely walk between the factories and back around the road. Paula talked to me all the time. She told me about her dog, an Alsatian who had gone over the rainbow bridge on New Year's Day. Her voice went funny as she told me this, and her cheeks were wet. She picked me up for a cuddle, and I licked the wet from her cheeks: it was very salty but made Paula smile again, which made me happy, too. I liked Paula, she was lovely. But we didn't see the fox.

I soon found out that we went to work every day. I began to like it as I got to meet lots of people who wanted to give me cuddles and let me lick them! Some even brought me nice treats, but I needed to be choosy; biscuit ones shaped like bones were boring, and there was no meat! I was a special dog, and I liked meaty treats.

Every day, Paula came in and took me for a walk, and she kept a secret stash of treats just for me in her pocket, usually a bit of ham or beef from her sandwiches. I liked walking with Paula; she talked to me about everything, which was nice. I didn't understand her, but I wanted to hear her talking. I liked it more when we stood chatting on the corner as there were lovely bacon and sausage smells from the Corner Café. I wondered if she would go in and get me a sausage, but she never did. Sometimes, we went into another shop for a chat; this made me sneeze as it was a florist, but I got lots of cuddles from the ladies in there and sometimes a nice treat, too.

Paula said she had to go to the bank one day, so we set off in a different direction. There were lots of new smells and people stopping to say hello to me and have a fuss. I saw a big dog across the road and barked; he was big and dark, and I was fearful.

When we got to the bank, they had magic doors! They opened without Paula touching them; how clever was that? But, before we could get too far, we were stopped by a man in a suit. He wouldn't let me in! Dogs were not allowed in the bank, and Paula was not happy. She persuaded him to let her make her transaction, and we left with Paula walking very quickly. She had a very red face and was muttering to herself, so I only caught the word stupid. I thought I had done something wrong, but when we went around the corner, Paula sat on a wall and picked me up for a cuddle. I started wagging my tail. It must have been the man in the suit that she was mad at. I was happy.

Paula said she was taking me to a special place next. I wondered where as we walked along the street-lots of legs and shopping bags on wheels, lots of children and lots of smells. I could smell meat again...ah, butchers, my favourite. We were not going in there, but the shop we went into smelled nice. It smelt like where I had been with Shemom, and there were those boffy things. A big smiley man helped Paula buy some chewy stuff: they were treats for me! She bent down to me and said, "Joey, this is our secret; don't let Shemom know I've spoiled you."

I was so happy I barked and wagged my tail really, really hard!

Chapter Ten

I was nervous. Very nervous. I was about to do something new for the both of us: dog training classes. We were to attend puppy training, and I had no idea how we would get along with other dogs. I knew I had to do something about Joey's barking and agitation in the car.

I'd tried having him in the front with me, but all he wanted to do was get my hand on his head and sit on my lap, as well as whining constantly. I'd tried him in the back, but he paced around barking and tried to get into the front. If I solved this issue, we would avoid the chance of ending up in a crash. I'd tried stopping along the route, wondering if he wanted a pee, but no. I'd tried toys and chews to no avail. He would not stop barking for the whole journey, and I was getting agitated.

After paying the initial visit, where Joey sat under my chair, I enrolled us in their puppy training class. This was after explaining to the trainer what our problems were. It was to the surprise of the other people when I walked in with Joey: yes, he looked young, but not puppy-like.

We managed to join the queue to register, with Joey acting as the perfect pet. He didn't bark or lunge at other dogs. He got fussed by a few people and welcomed by the trainer. Then I saw the three Shelties wagging their tails under the table where we were to book in. Oh lord, was he going to have a go at them, as there were three this time, not two? I reined him in tightly and juggled his vaccination card and payment.

I relaxed, only to find Joey, in a typical dog manner, had snuck under the table and had his nose up the bum of one of the Shelties. All three were brushed to within an inch of their life, and their coats stood long and proud. All three stood facing their owner, with their bums on display for all to see. Joey moved from one to the other, and none of them turned or took any notice; what a relief! I called him away to sit on our own so I could relax; my nerves were jangling, and Joey soon took solace on my lap.

There were about a dozen dogs, from scruffy mongrels to Schnauzers, all puppies, apart from Joey. Thankfully, Joey had not barked at any of them. Peter welcomed us and introduced himself and the team before explaining what we would do that evening: basic walking at heel, sit and stay—sounded good to me. Although Joey was well trained in walking, he rarely walked to heel, preferring to do the nose-down-the-ground zigzag of a scenting Spaniel, which could trip me up if I wasn't mindful. After being instructed on how to hold the lead properly, we formed a circle about a dog's length apart and began to walk around the hall.

I couldn't help but laugh at the tiny Shih-Tzus, who were so fluffy that you couldn't tell which end was which, being scooted along like mops on the plastic covering the floor. Meanwhile, Joey was busy looking around at the other dogs again. He was gaining confidence as we paraded around and had his eyes on a standard poodle puppy. Six months old and full size, it was lolloping around with confidence.

Woof, woof, woof, oh no, Joey was off. One tug on the lead, and I was lunging inwards as he shot towards the other dog. He may only have been nine kilos, but when the will took him, he had the strength of a lion. I pulled him back and shushed him. *Woof*, went the poodle, *yap*, from a Pekinese. I felt my face redden as Joey started the dog chorus again. Nooo! His tail wagged, and his head held proudly aloft; he enjoyed being the centre of attention and would not be quiet. Meanwhile, Peter was in the circle's centre with his Great Dane, who ignored them all. Peter came over and persuaded Joey to be silent; at least he could now see the problem.

Once order was restored, we continued around the room and moved on to turn correctly, with the dog keeping close at heel. I started to relax and kept Joey concentrating on the task. Thank heavens for keeping treats in my pocket. Then we went on to make the dogs sit. In the short time I had had Joey, I hadn't requested he sit. As long as he stood still at the kerb, I wasn't of a mind to make him sit in a puddle. This would be a new challenge or a breeze.

It wasn't a breeze. We were advised to use the command 'sit' and gently but firmly place our hand on the dog's rear to indicate our intent. We were instructed to walk around again, turn at heel and issue the command. The walking went well; the turn went well, but the sit? Joey looked at me and blinked. My hand went to his rear end, and I repeated the command. The bum became immovable. I tried again. The hand was in place, and the whole of his body went rigid; he was having none of it. The treats came out: vocal command, hand on rear, treat in front of the nose. Joey stood solid, and the treat was devoured. Hmmm.

It seemed I needed help. Peter came over and tried, only to receive a sneer from Joey and a firm refusal. He told me to persevere. I tried again. Sneer. I was getting flustered. A smiling lady [minus a dog] came walking over.

"Can I help?" she gave Joey a fuss, "try this."

She crouched down, treat in one hand, and an interested Joey gazing at her. With her other arm, she raised her hand from horizontal up to vertical and repeated the command to sit. He sat and got a treat. She did it again, and Joey was rewarded. She gave me a treat, and I sat. I didn't, but I was so wrapped up in training that I felt I should. I followed the signals and command, and by Jove, he sat! I beamed, and Joey stayed sitting with his tail swishing, awaiting more treats.

A weary owner and an excited dog left that first dog

training session. My nerves were still jangling, but we had accomplished something at least.

Chapter Eleven

One thing puppy training didn't teach Joey was his party piece. He was an ace flycatcher. I was quietly sitting in the conservatory reading when I heard jaws snap. I looked at Joey; he looked at me, then unceremoniously spat out a fly. I thought this was a one-off, but it became a regular occurrence. He would even jump from the chair he was sitting on and catch them mid-flight to the opposite chair. This didn't always go to plan. Sometimes, he missed the fly; other times, he missed the chair and plopped onto the floor. That move was one to be discouraged, so the chairs got rearranged!

His other favourite thing in the conservatory was watching the neighbour's cats. It was a regular game between them that they would tease Joey into a chase when they were outside. They would lure him to the bottom of the garden and then quickly head back up to the top with him in hot pursuit. They would leap up and over the garden fence when he was inches away, leaving a frustrated and panting Joey sitting there wondering what had happened. They would sit on the garden fence staring at him, knowing full well that they were safe from him getting to them.

My house was semi-detached, with the back door on the side of the building. The previous owners had made a covered walkway to the back garden, a handy space for storage. The cats sauntered along the fence, sat on the roof of this walkway and proceeded to clean themselves. Joey would sense they were there, jump onto a chair, then sit rigidly, watching them watch him. Cats certainly know exactly how to tease dogs.

One of the first decent walks I went on with Joey was down to the local cemetery. I was an occasional photographer and thought it would be a nice walk for him with interesting sniffs, and I could take some photos, too.

I had bought an extending lead so he could have a decent amount of freedom when we were in a suitable area. We trotted off with many pauses for Joey to be fussed by various people. He loved it.

The cemetery goes back to 1854 and covers twelve acres, much of which is mature woodland, so it was a pleasant place to wander around for Joey and a lot of history to uncover in the old gravestones for me. What I hadn't bargained for was the plethora of squirrels who lived there.

Joey was sniffing up a tree, and I was setting the focus on my camera. The birds were singing, and all was tranquil in our world.

Hmmm, what's Shemom doing fiddling with that black thing?

SQUIRREL!

I was focused in seconds.

I forgot all about Shemom as I watched the squirrel running past me. Oh, there's another one: which way should I go? I momentarily paused as I decided which way to go before I shot off. I barked and ran to the left, glanced at the other squirrel, changed direction and went right. All I could hear was the whizz of the lead as I got further away from Shemom. Then my lead went tight. I pulled again but couldn't get at the blasted squirrels now as they had run up the trees!

Woof, woof, woof. My paws were up on the tree. My tail was wagging in excitement. The squirrel I could see was in the next branch up, and he just sat there blinking at me.

"JOEY!"

Sorry, I'm not taking my eyes off this squirrel. I want to get it!

"JOEY!"

Shemom's tone was urgent, so I turned to look. Where was she? I looked around before my eyes followed the red of my extending lead. What was she doing face down on the floor?

"Joey, get here now!"

While concentrating on the camera, I didn't realise Joey had spotted the squirrels. His jerk on the lead at speed had me off balance. As I stepped forward to regain my balance, I tripped over a tree root, tumbling onto the ground amongst damp, half-mulched leaves. Thankfully, I had the camera strap around my neck, but as I fell, it bashed me on the nose. I grappled around for my lens cap and gingerly stood up. I was covered in muddy leaves and winced when I touched my nose.

I had managed to keep hold of Joey's lead, though. Now back on two feet, I reeled him in and decided we had had enough of an adventure for today. Hoping I didn't look like Stig of the Dump, we headed our way back home. Lesson to self: don't take the camera and Joey out simultaneously.

Chapter Twelve

I was getting used to this new life but still wanted to go home. How long would I be staying here? Okay, it was comfortable. I was allowed on the furniture; I slept on a very cosy bed and was fed good food. When I say good food, it took a long while before Shemom got the right one. I'm a special boy, and no cheap stuff suited my palate; it had to be the correct tin of yumminess. Only by refusing to eat would I get my message across. After changing brands, Shemom finally got there, and as long as she didn't put too many biscuits in, I was happy.

It was going to be a late-into-work day. The joy of being self-employed was that you could be flexible on hours to a degree. Usually, though, it was more early in and late leave when I was busy. I rarely gave myself time off: I was too strict with myself. Of course, the other benefit was taking Joey to work with me. When you are single, a self-employed lifestyle doesn't work in your favour if you have a pet who can't be with you.

I was even enjoying being in the car. Now that I knew I wouldn't be returned to the kennels, I trusted Mom to take good care of me. I hadn't tried to run away for ages.

Oops, did I call her mom?

Where were we off in the car today? I had only put my head down for a snooze when we stopped: that was quick! Lead on, and I jumped from the car. I knew I had been here before and quickly realised I was near where I had met the boppy bunnies. Woohoo, I was going to play.

Well, I was wrong there. Mom led me into a different door. Hmmm. This place was bright and smelt of dogs, cats and antiseptic. Ugh. We were at the vet: we had been here a few days ago when the vet jabbed me and looked at my teeth. Oh well, although I wouldn't say I liked being poked and prodded, I was always back out of here in a few minutes. Mom sat down, and I settled between her legs. A place I felt safe and secure, especially when a woman with a horse on a lead came in. It was a Great Dane like Peter's dog at puppy class, but to me, it was massive. I scooted back so he couldn't see me, but then got worried and jumped onto Mom's lap. He didn't seem so scary now I was higher up. He was being a wuss and was whining and giving little grumble barks. He obviously didn't like the vets, either!

A pretty young lady called my name, and I wagged my tail as she came towards me. I was going to get treats and fuss, I was sure. But hang on, what's going on? Mom gave her my lead, and we went through another door! I was scared and wished I hadn't taken the mickey out of the Great Dane. Mind you, I can't see anyone carrying him in through that door! This young lady was talking to me, and

I began to relax. She popped me on a lovely, cosy towel, and then I seemed to have gone to sleep.

I hated leaving Joey at the vet. We had spent very little time apart, but his teeth were awful and desperate for a clean with the possibility of one extraction. One of his canine teeth was horribly black, and the vet said it may have to come out.

I went to work, minus my little buddy, and awaited the vet's call. My concentration levels were minimal, so it was a good day to tidy and organise paperwork. I couldn't help but look at the clock every five minutes.

I knew I wouldn't get a call until after 2 pm, so I tried not to be too stressed. I don't like it when I'm not in control of something; even though I trust the professionals, it's still a worry.

By 2:30 pm, I could no longer stand it; my office area was neat as a pin, and the bin overflowed. I'd not eaten any lunch as my stomach was in knots. I transferred the landline to my mobile, locked up, and headed home. I had just got in the door when the phone rang.

"Hi Alison, Joey is ready to go home now."

I sighed with relief.

"Great, I'll be with you in five minutes."

"All went well, with his teeth clean and no extractions," the receptionist said. "One of the girls has gone to fetch him, and here's your bill."

I gulped at the £200 plus bill, paid and then waited for my boy to appear. The door opened, and I heard his name being called.

Oh my, I want to go back to sleep! I have no idea what

just happened, but I feel very unsteady. I licked my lips. Hang on, my mouth feels different, and my teeth are all shiny and smooth. Hmmm.

"Joey, come on now. It's time to go home."

I blinked up at the pretty girl, and then I saw Mom. With extreme effort, I put one foot in front of the other and slowly and very uncertainly made my way towards Mom. She was down on the floor to greet me and was laughing. Yeah, okay, I can't walk straight at the minute, but I'll be fine. I tried to wag my tail, but only the white tip would obey my command. Mom was cuddling me now. Oh, it felt so good. I leant into her, and my tail wagged properly.

"Can we go home now, Mom, please? I want to sleep."

I made slow, wobbly progress to the car, and Mom sat me in the front. I licked her hand in appreciation. Within minutes, we were home, and after a drink of water, I settled on the chair and my favourite fluffy cushion and went back to sleep.

Thanks, Mom.

Having Joey back with me was a relief. I knew his teeth were good for a few more years, and his breath was so much fresher. It didn't take long for the anaesthetic to wear off, and, of course, he wanted food. For the first time, he cleared his bowl of biscuits and meat. Let's hope that continues.

The following morning, it was like nothing had happened. A very happy, waggy Joey woke me up by walking all over me. Refreshed from his long sleeping sessions, he decided that if he was awake, I should be too, even at 7 am on a Saturday.

With my dressing gown on, we went downstairs, and I let him out while making a cup of tea. With Joey suitably widdled, I decided to return to bed and read. Joey zoomed off ahead of me and plopped himself on the bed. It was okay with him, too!

It was good to feel normal again, and when we went back to the place called work, lots of people came in to see me as they knew I had been to the doggy doctor [I hated the word vet.] Micky Muppet came in every day if we hadn't been into his work unit to see him and Papa Smurf.

Both of them were lovely and fussed over me a lot. Micky Muppet was tall and was always smiling; he often brought my mom treats of chocolate bars or scones with sweet jam and cream. Papa Smurf was shorter and balding and, apart from not being blue, looked like Papa Smurf! They were mechanics, and their work unit always smelt strange: oil and stuff! But I didn't care. I got lots and lots of cuddles and fuss. Even Paula used to take me in to see them during our lunchtime walks. I enjoyed meeting all these people, and they always smiled. Paula told me I made everyone happy, especially my mom. She said Mom was a different person now that I was around, that she was much more content. I admit, so was I, even though I missed not having a dad.

Chapter Thirteen

Once Joey would sit for treats, I decided to see if this approach worked in the car. If Joey were quiet, life would be much less stressful for me and, undoubtedly, for him. Yes, the training sessions were working, but it was still a work in progress.

I'd never had a dog so vocal when travelling, but I suppose noise outweighs the thought of him being sick. Ugh. I purchased small treats to keep in the car. Joey had his harness put on, and I rattled the bag of treats once he was in the car to get him to sit. He sat. He received a small treat. All was quiet, so I set off to work.

He whined; I commanded him to sit. He sat and was quiet for a nanosecond. The command to be quiet had no effect. More whining, he began nudging my hand when I was changing gears. I took no notice, so he started barking. My first big mistake: I gave him a treat. This wasn't going to work. It didn't take me long to realise I was encouraging bad behaviour: now I had to get him out of wanting treats by barking.

I reverted to Joey travelling in the back of the van, and that was worse. My van was a tiny Peugeot with a wire mesh between the front seats and the loading space. So once in, he would be clipped in for safety and still have enough space to move around. But the minute he was there, he paced the floor and barked. I would be deaf if he carried on like this, but at least he wasn't pawing at me.

What next, I wondered. I went off to the local large pet store and purchased a crate. Thankfully, Joey was only a small dog, but a small cage was too small; a medium, providing it fit in, was just suitable. The slight spanner in the works was that the only crate I could get had only one door. As the crate would be across the van's width, Joey had to be lifted into the tailgate and then persuaded to enter the door on the side.

But my first problem was different from what I expected. I couldn't get it in the van in its flat-pack box. I sighed. There was nothing for it but to extract the crate from the packaging in the middle of a busy car park with people expecting me to move out of the space so that they could claim it. A broken nail or two later, I opened the packaging, unfolded the crate in its space, and folded the packaging on top. It was a tight fit, but it was in. The next hurdle would be getting Joey in it!

I tried it out with a blanket in the base, a favourite toy, and some treats to encourage him.

He entered as sweet as anything: result! But what

would happen once we moved off? There was only one way to find out.

He barked. Then he barked some more before whining. I took a few small treats and twisted my arm back between the seats, fingers through the cage mesh divider and then to his cage. It wasn't ideal driving, I know. Treats were issued, but he still wouldn't settle. However, he stayed relatively calm for the rest of the journey, and I was less stressed when we got to work. Go, Team Joey, for making progress, I thought. When we reached our destination, I had his lead ready to clip on when I opened the crate door and allowed him out.

This was fine until we arrived at work one morning a week or two later. I parked up and opened the tailgate. Joey wagged his tail and barked. With the clip on his lead ready to attach, I opened the crate door for him to step out. As he did so, he caught a scent in the air and tried to leap from the van before his lead was on. Thankfully, I grabbed his collar before he could run off, but with his nose twitching madly, I could only assume that Mr Fox had recently passed by. I'd have to be very careful with that one.

Whilst we continued training classes, we both continued to be stressed at some point during the session. By and large, Joey got on with most of the other dogs now, but there were a few he just reacted to by barking or growling if any of them got too close. Those that managed to get into his space that he disliked would receive a nip as he backed away to the safety of my legs. The dogs he didn't seem to like were always large and dark-coloured that would loom over him. I wondered what had happened in his past to make him fear bigger, dark dogs.

When our six weeks of training were almost complete, we were a little more relaxed and working together, but the one thing I couldn't summon up the courage to do was sit, stay, come. Leaving Joey to his own devices whilst I stepped a few paces away was, I felt, too much of a temptation for him to head straight off to the other dogs he disliked and have a go at them. I did not want that to happen.

For this part of the session, the class sat at one end of the room, and a trainer, dog owner, and dog moved to the other. Those who had done this bit already had done a great job, but I now felt under pressure for us to succeed. I explained my concerns to the trainer, and she said that we could use a long training lead. If Joey decided to divert from the proceedings, we could step on the lead before he got to the other end.

Happy with that, I removed my jacket and flung it across to the side of the room and out of the way. The trainer called Joey across to her, encouraged him to sit for a treat and praised him. Now, it was my turn to urge him to return to me.

I took a deep breath and issued the command to come. Well, he did in a fashion. His nose was on overdrive, and he diverted via my jacket pocket to get a treat before coming to me.

He was almost as good as gold; at least he ignored the other dogs.

In those six weeks, we had made progress. Joey, aged

ten years old, had completed puppy training, and we proudly left with a certificate and a rosette. Personally, I needed another six weeks to relax: I had found the training very tiring and stressful. But we had left with some solid techniques and renewed hope that all would be well if we kept it up.

Chapter Fourteen

I followed the dog trainer's advice with Joey and successfully trained him to lie down, wait, and leave. The one thing that Joey wouldn't do was come when he was called. As he didn't do this in the garden or on a training lead in an open space, I was not risking letting him off unless we were in a secure area.

He still tended to want to escape whenever he could, and I had no idea why. By now, I thought he would have settled into his new home.

A friend came to stop for the weekend, and we ordered a curry to be delivered. The doorbell rang, something Joey ignored, and I went into the hall, closing the lounge door behind me.

"Good evening, your takeaway order," said a smiling man. "That'll be..." He looked at the bill.

"Oh damn, I've left the money inside, one moment."

I pushed the front door almost closed just as my friend slightly opened the lounge door to pass me the money. It was the smallest of gaps: enough to get my hand through. But that gap was enough, and Joey was through it like a lightning bolt. He barged past the delivery driver, ran up the front drive to the main road, and dived into the traffic.

"JOEY!"

With the money for the curry scattered across the hall floor, I ran up the drive, leaving the delivery driver somewhat dazed by this flash of black and white that had whooshed past him. It was dark, and Joey was mostly black: it was a recipe for disaster. With beeps of horns from passing traffic, Joey ran straight across the road and back again, heading down a neighbour's drive and into her open garage. I was trying not to panic.

Slowly and carefully, I walked down her driveway. When I caught up with him, he was happily sniffing around, absorbed in the scent he had tracked. The neighbour kept ferrets, so this was an exciting scent for Joey. He was not impressed to be lifted from his sensory activity before being carried back home. My friend had picked up the cash and paid off the delivery driver and was now standing there, not knowing what had happened or what to do. It had all happened so fast!

Joey was so unimpressed with me that he climbed onto my friend's lap and the back of the chair once we had eaten. He lay there scowling at me for some time before going to sleep. I was not a popular mom.

As Joey was now quite happy snuffling around in the back garden, I would open the door and leave him to it. Allowing dogs to get their sensory pleasure in the garden and on walks is essential. I hate to see anyone walking their dog and dragging them away from lampposts and walls. The sniffing is as crucial to the dog as having a pee. The garden was pretty secure, with fencing and hedging all around. Much to his disappointment, any gaps had been closed off as soon as he found them.

While cooking, I realised that Joey had been outside for quite some time. My house was at the top of a hill with the back garden falling away. From the conservatory, I had a good view of the whole garden. I looked out the window and couldn't spot him, so I wondered what he was doing. I called his name; nothing. I walked down the garden, looking behind bushes and under them. I looked behind the shed, but still nothing. Where the heck had he gone? There were no doors to the front, so he must be here somewhere. I doubted if he had come past me in the kitchen and gone inside. I searched the house and still a big fat nothing. I looked out the back bedroom window and finally saw him in the neighbour's garden!

He had been nosing around one spot in the hedge previously, but as there was a mesh fence there, I didn't worry about it. Running back downstairs, I went to the spot in the hedge. He had worked his way through the hedge and got through the mesh! There he was, happily patrolling the garden along with the neighbour's dog, Flash.

I called the neighbour and asked her to come out the back, and she was stunned to see Joey there with Flash, both with tails wagging as if it were normal. Off I went around to hers to remove Joey, who was, once more, not impressed. To Joey's disgust, the hole was blocked up in the hedge. But within a week, he had worked himself another hole and was back in there again! I needed a better solution than blocking holes as he made them.

I went to the local hardware store, bought a roll of six-inch square mesh fence, squashed it into the privet hedge, and secured it. I got that look of disappointment from him again. This time, it took him about four weeks to work out how to worm his way under and through and back to his mate, Flash. Underneath all his Sheltie floof, Joey was a slim dog, no bigger than a good-sized cat. I started to look at things from that angle; if a cat could get through, then so could Joey.

I learnt that he was up to no good if he was out for a pee for too long!

I needed mesh with smaller holes, so I went to the hardware store again to view their netting rolls. I could only secure the garden by ripping out the hedging and replacing it with fencing. This was not in my budget!

They had four types of mesh fencing: one I could get my foot through, a six-inch one I knew was useless, strawberry netting that would rip, and a black, one-inch square one. Now, that looked promising. It was also quite pliable, so I could shape it into the hedge and secure it easier. Thankfully, it wasn't expensive either. Let's hope I could get it secured and that it worked.

Joey followed me down the garden with interest as I lugged the twelve meters of fencing with me and unrolled it. He sniffed. He prodded, then finally walked over to it and cocked his leg up it: that's what he thought of that, then!

I pushed and shoved the mesh into place, and Joey watched with interest as the holes of his previous escapes were covered up. Within minutes the clever little bugger managed to get his nose underneath and then his head. He promptly felt my hands around his middle and was dragged back into the garden before he could get any further through. This guy was too smart for his own good.

I sat back on my heels. How the heck was I going to stop my little Houdini? I had an idea. Being a lifelong camper, I wasn't short of tent pegs and a mallet. I went into the shed and unearthed them.

What is she doing? She's lying on MY grass and shoving this black stuff into MY hedge. How am I supposed to visit my buddy Flash now? I'll have to find another way to get through. Ooh, great, she's gone into the shed; let me see what I can do. Yup, I can nose this up, and there's a gap I can get through. I'm sorted for later. Now, wouldn't be a good idea.

What has she got now? A black bag rattled as she returned towards the new mesh, and she tipped out a load of metal spikey things. Good grief, what were those for? I was confused.

Mom grabbed one and pushed it through the black mesh and into the ground. She did this a few more times before sitting back. She looked at me.

"Try that then, Joey; you won't get through there in a rush."

Well, I was happy to oblige!

With a wag of the tail, I went to the bottom of the mesh and put my nose under it. It wouldn't budge. I tried again. Damn, she really had fixed it.

Feeling annoyed, I decided to go and lie inside and think about this. It was not on!

I could continue spreading the mesh down the garden hedge with Joey out of the way. My knees were killing me. I made good progress and managed to do the whole side of the garden over the next hour or so. Not without getting stung by stingers and scratched by brambles. It was a small price to pay for the peace of mind it would give me. If I allowed the hedge to grow through the mesh, anchoring it even better. I would have to constantly remind myself not to go too mad with the hedge cutter, as you could barely see the mesh! I made a mental note to monitor his favourite places before sitting down for a rest and a cup of tea.

I hadn't banked on Joey changing sides in the garden and going into stealth mode to get through to the neighbours on the other side. Most of that side was fenced, with only a privet hedge of about ten feet at the top. I had blocked off all the gaps I had seen him go towards and was confident we were secure. Wrong.

Once more, he was out for longer than expected, so I went to check. He emerged with a rustle of privet hedge, gave me a sideways glare, and headed indoors. I was fed up. Would Joey ever settle here and not be constantly trying to escape? Another hole blocked up and a very disgruntled dog. I was getting used to the sneering look he gave me when I found his escape holes.

What worried me most about getting into this neighbour's garden was that they had three Border Terriers who barked like mad when coming outside. I was afraid that they and Joey would end up in an argument. The following day, another trip to the hardware store for more mesh. Belt and braces approach this time.

The family with the Border Terriers hadn't lived there long and were making lovely improvements to the house. Much-needed hacking was required in the rear garden. As the property had previously been a rental, the garden was left to look after itself. This was a shame, as it had been a lovely old-fashioned style garden with crazy paving paths and well-tended shrubs when I had moved in. I had kept the hedging on both sides of my garden down to a manageable height, even though neither belonged to me. But over the years, as I'd gotten older and busier, I couldn't do it anymore, so their hedge had grown like mad. They worked hard on their garden. Loads of creeping ivy were pulled out, especially at the bottom, where it wound around a tree trunk. Hedges were butchered back down to a reasonable height and thinned out.

It was a Groundhog Day moment when Joey failed to come in again. Out I went, and he was nowhere to be seen. I checked all my mesh and returned to the house to see if he had slipped past me. He had a habit of going to bed when he felt like it, but he wasn't there.

Back in the garden, I saw pawprints in mud and sawdust at the side of the shed. I hadn't seen this as a problem due to the thick pyracantha by the side of the shed. The little beggar had made a tunnel under the pyracantha, gone around the back, and dropped down into the garden at the back!

"JOEY!"

A rustle: he was there somewhere, but I couldn't squeeze into the gap to see. Worried about where he would end up, I headed out the door, lead in hand, to visit the neighbour. My heart was beating like crazy. I popped my head into the corner shop and asked them to keep an eye out for him and grab him if they could, should he appear.

There was no answer at the house, but they had an open side leading to the garden, so I walked through to see if Joey was there. I called his name again, but nothing. The adjoining neighbour had heard me shouting and came out of his door.

"You lost your dog?"

"Yes, have you seen him?"

"Yes, he's wandering around in my back garden; come on through."

I headed through only to find Joey gone. But I did see the tip of a tail going into the hedge to the previous garden. I ran around to see him standing there, looking at me and wondering what all the fuss was about. Then he headed for another hedge. I went back to the neighbouring house and into the back garden. No Joey. My stress levels were going off the scale. Had he gone back home?

Back home, I opened the door and scoured the garden, but nothing. Where could he be? I raced upstairs to see nothing from the window into the neighbour's garden. My neighbour was on holiday, and I couldn't see fully around the whole garden: there was only one thing for it. Thankfully, I had a set of keys for emergencies. This was an emergency. Feeling somewhat guilty, I let myself in, entered their kitchen and unlocked the backdoor; Joey was waiting to come in. Once more, he was unfazed by all the anguish he had caused. Lead on, I took him back home.

Next? Yes, you've guessed it: more mesh and more blocking off! I'd had ten months of Joey adventures and was a nervous wreck!

Chapter Fifteen

Mom did not understand that I had to explore. After all, a trait of the Sheltie is to herd, and the delicately powerful scenting nose of the Cocker Spaniel is to scent their prey. As a mix of the two breeds, these things alone meant my nose ruled my head and paws. I was a Super Sniffer! New smells around me MUST be investigated, unearthed, and dealt with unless they were slugs or frogs... ugh.

Holes in hedges were meant to be explored.

Doors ajar were meant to go through.

No amount of walking on a lead would fully satisfy my curiosity. And why should I come back when I knew where I was going and what I was doing? Those car things on the road held no fear for me, but they made Mom freak out, and she drove one!

She did let me off in a park once. I don't know why, but it never happened again. I mean. I did come back... eventually.

We seemed to be getting along okay. Mom treated me well, and the image of Dad faded into a pleasant memory. I was fed nice food, allowed on the furniture and the bed [result!], and never left alone for too long. I couldn't complain.

One Sunday afternoon, Mom put my lead on well before walkies time. I wondered where we were going. Mom had only just been chatting over the hedge out the back where the Border Terriers lived, and as quick as you like, she had my lead in her hand.

We went up the path and turned left to go on our regular walk, but she turned left again and down the Terrier's driveway. What was happening here? She rattled the side gate, and as we waited, I felt Mom tense up. Why? They're only other dogs, and I'd met them before when I snuck through the fence for a poo!

Through the garden gate we went, and I was let off. I quickly found myself nose-to-nose with Pippa, Pudsey and Bruno, the three Border Terriers. Pudsey sniffed and walked away uninterested. Bruno sniffed and made his way to my bum. Oy, mate! And the third? Pippa gave me a low growl. She was the boss then! Suitably admonished by her owner, she too turned away, and I trotted forward to explore and ignore everyone else.

The Borders were just as unimpressed as I was with the meeting, and we crisscrossed around the garden sniffing bums and peeing on each other's noses if they got in the way. But blimey, these guys were noisy! Toss a small round thing, and they were yapping away like someone had thrown a meat carcass their way! I didn't know what they were doing with this round thing, but they seemed to enjoy it. I just went across to Carl, jumped up on the bench, and then, on his lap for a cuddle. Carl gave great cuddles, and I rewarded him with lots of kisses.

Chapter Sixteen

It was almost time for me to head off to Spain for a week, and I had a dog sitter coming to live in while I was away. It was my next-door neighbour's daughter. I felt much happier than putting Joey into kennels: I wasn't sure we were ready for that experience.

In truth, I was reluctant to leave him with anyone, but he loved Emily, and I knew she would dote on him whilst I was away. The fridge and freezer were full of food for her, and Joey had enough treats to last him a month! With some trepidation, I left for the airport.

Throughout the week, I had regular 'pupdates' on social media. Joey went for lovely long walks and was generally spoiled to death. Emily was happy taking Joey to bed with her and encouraged him to curl up under the duvet! Let's hope that didn't become a habit he wanted to continue.

A few years before getting Joey, I had bought a small

townhouse on the edge of the Sierra Nevada in Lanjaron, Spain. I planned to go and live there. I went over every couple of months and built up some good friends there, both Spanish and English. It was a great little town to relax in. I had a wonderful week in the sunshine, catching up with my friends in the village. I loved being in my second home. It was a sleepy town in the Alpujarra's, far from the tourist coastal towns. I was part of the community, even if my Spanish was awful. I enjoyed the relaxed atmosphere and the fact that going for a loaf of bread could take five minutes to an hour, depending on who you met. A quick hello was rare; a stop for a coffee or a small beer was the norm. I won't tell you how often I went out for one thing and returned with nothing as I forgot what I'd originally gone out for. I could be out for hours, even when I was decorating and popping out in my scuffs to the *ferretería* [hardware store] for supplies; there was usually someone who wanted to stop for a chat so we could catch up on the local gossip. For such a small village, there was always something going on.

It was different from your typical tourist destination as it was a thirty-minute drive from the coast, but it did attract Spanish tourists to its Spa at the end of town. The waters from the Sierra Nevada ran into over twenty-one fountains in the town, and the minerals were said to have healing properties. I loved going there for its tranquillity, beautiful views from the small terrace, and lack of commercialism.

I daydreamed about how much I was looking forward to living here in the future, and I was sure Joey would adore it, too. Most people had adopted dogs that were rescued from living on the street. I missed having Joey to curl up to and wondered if he was missing me, too.

On the return flight, I was feeling refreshed. I was impatient to get through customs at Birmingham Airport and get to my car. I was desperate to see the boy. Thankfully, I only travelled light with hand luggage, so I didn't have to wait at the baggage carousel. I weaved through people standing and waiting for the carousel to move, and nipped into the toilet, before heading for the green channel. A blast of cold air hit me as I went outside, and I walked swiftly off towards the car park. The wheels on my small case bounced around in the ruts of the paving slabs, narrowly avoiding my ankles as I walked. Case thrown onto the backseat, I started the car, headed through the barrier and reminded myself which side of the road I needed to drive on. The M42 was, as ever, busy but thankfully moving.

When I opened the front door, I was lovingly pounced upon by a perfectly intact and happy Joey. Evidently, he had taken a liking to pizza. Really? I found this odd as Joey had never begged or had scraps. It transpired that Emily had worked a double shift, cooked pizza, and then fallen asleep on the sofa, leaving the leftovers on the plate on the floor. Joey thought it was fair game to steal the pepperoni. I hoped it didn't have an adverse effect on his rear end!

Emily looked after Joey several times whilst I went to Lanjaron, much to his delight, but I needed to get kennels sorted for when she wasn't available. I turned to social media and got recommended a local small business with a lady called Nicky.

I took Joey to meet her and was shown around. Joey had his halo perfectly poised that day and didn't put a paw wrong. He was angelic, and Nicky and Lisa, the groomer, fell immediately in love with him. I left feeling happy that he would be well cared for. I just hoped he would behave when I dropped him off in a few weeks.

I was stressing before I even got to the kennels. I'd never left a dog in a kennel because we rarely holidayed abroad. But now that I had a small bolt hole in Spain, I was a regular traveller. I hoped he didn't cause any issues. I was dreading a call from Nicky to say that he was a pain in the bum and needed to go. This was all down to all the barking and nipping he did with dogs he didn't like. My week in Spain was marred only by my concerns over him.

When I returned, I texted Nicky and headed straight from the airport to pick him up.

"How has he been?"

"Oh, he's been as good as gold; let me go and fetch him."

I waited in the grooming room for him to appear. He came trotting in, ignored me, and went straight to Lisa, the groomer!

"Joey, come here, boy."

His head turned, and he realised it was me. With a guilty wag, he jumped up into my arms.

"You didn't miss me at all, did you?" I said as I scratched behind his ears.

"He has been no trouble at all. He's stayed mostly in

the garden, sitting with me whilst I did some gardening," Nicky said. "Of a night he slept in the conservatory with my three. Although he tried to sleep on the sofa, my eldest dog soon turfed him off as that's his spot."

I couldn't believe I had worried for nothing.

Chapter Seventeen

Joey had settled much better after training, hopefully realising that he was with me for good. But I felt guilty when I left him behind to go to Spain. I knew he was well cared for and enjoyed all the fuss and attention he received, but it didn't stop me from feeling that he was missing out on holidays, too.

I'd grown up camping, and I had previously had a campervan before I bought my little place in Spain. I thought that going camping again would be nice. I wasn't getting any younger, but I felt a small tent was ideal for us to get away for a few nights during the summer. I could cope with the aches and pains of sleeping on a camp bed rather than a proper mattress.

There was no way we could manage in one of those tiny one-person tents shaped like a nylon triangular bar of chocolate, so I got a four-person tent with three flexible poles that I could easily erect. Let's see how that goes, then. I was excited about my purchase. Having been brought up going away in my family's touring caravan, I loved the British countryside.

Mom had this small green bundle of fabric and was going down to the flatter end of the garden with it. I wondered what she was going to do. I followed her down and lay on the grass to watch. She laid it down and unzipped the bag. Inside was more material and some poles. Oh, could it be some agility stuff cos that looked fun? The material was unfurled and was full of zips and bits of bright yellow cord. I sniffed at it...not that pleasant; it smelt new. Then, a long black thing bounced over my head. It was like a huge boingy magic wand. Then Mom cussed as it got caught in the hedge; what was she doing?

Maybe she was pointing out something in the hedge that I needed to investigate. There were now three of these boingy magic wands, and they were huge. Mom began threading them through the material, and, like magic, they were curving! Suddenly, this thing popped up into a green cave; this was kinda cool. I followed Mom inside, and she stood there smiling. Obviously, this green thing pleased her. I sniffed around; it needed to have my mark on it. There was a bit of material flapping. I sniffed, cocked my leg, and christened, what I was to learn, was called a tent. I'm unsure why Mom shouted at me for doing it, but I was pleased to have helped. She started removing the poles, and the tent went flat on the floor. Hmph, I bet she needs help folding this up. As she pulled and pushed the material around, I walked over it. I'm sure I was helpful, but Mom didn't seem to think so. It didn't take us long to roll it up and zip it back into the bag. But what was the point in putting it up and then taking it down again? This was as confusing as those balls I was supposed to enjoy.

Pleased that I could erect the tent on my own, I bought some essential camping cookware and a self-inflating mattress to go on top of the camp bed. I was going back to basics, but I needed some comfort. I already had a suitable sleeping bag. Now I just had to pluck up the courage to actually go somewhere!

It was more than twelve months before I used that tent. Even then, it wasn't in the way I had initially planned.

Basically, I chickened out. I could list many reasons, but two big things swayed me from being under canvas. One, I had always been in a caravan or campervan, with only a short spell in my late teens with a tent, and I vividly remember pumping up the airbed and, the following morning, waking to feel two sheep leaning against the tent onto my head. Two was Joey, his barking on site, and the fear of him doing one of his Houdini moves when I was asleep. [I'd had a previous dog do precisely that: she went off to scrounge sausages from other people before we got up!]

The solution came by way of a microcamper. I know, a contradiction in terms as most average campers aren't huge, but I needed to have something I could use every day but would also allow us to go camping. My budget and requirements led me to consider a Berlingo Urban Camper conversion. It had a nice comfy bed, sink and single burner cooker. What more could we want within my budget? At least I could sleep easy knowing we were both inside a safe environment without Joey escaping. I booked a few weekends away and packed Bertie [the Berlingo] with everything we needed.

Joey was pleased that his travel cage didn't fit in the back and was happily in his harness on the front seat. I threw in the unused tent, which would give us extra space if it wasn't warm enough to sit outside. It also made us look like real campers rather than a car parked on a pitch.

We headed to Winchcombe in the Cotswolds on a bright Friday afternoon, our first adventure. The electric cool box was filled with enough food for the weekend and several bottles of wine. Dried and tinned food was packed into a couple of neat plastic boxes fitted into one cupboard, and we were sorted.

I was incredibly nervous as we set off. My mind was in overdrive as to what could go wrong. Foremost was Joey being an annoying devil and barking constantly, especially while I was setting up. I'd picked this site primarily as I knew it had good dog walks and was generally quiet, as I had camped here before when I had a VW Trident. I knew we could have a pitch that wasn't surrounded by lots of people, so fewer people to annoy if Joey turned into the devil dog!

I pulled onto the site, feeling apologetic. My camper looked like a standard car. It caused much amusement at this point with the wardens, and they came out to take a look. I had booked a pitch by the lovely lake, but, due to recent wet weather, they had to move me right opposite reception on a giant pitch usually reserved for family tents. We looked lost and abandoned.

Joey was barking for attention and wondering what was going on, so I attached Joey to a ground anchor once I had plugged in the electrics. He could snuffle around whilst I put the kettle on and made a cup of tea. He had a drink of water and lay down, surveying his surroundings. Dare I say that he was quiet?

I grabbed the tent and unrolled it all. Joey lay still and watched. While the going was good, I got the tent up and linked the canopy across the side door of the Berlingo. I felt pretty smug that it had all gone so well, and Joey did not make a peep. I popped my bucket toilet into the awning out of the way and opened my camping chair. Still, Joey did not make a sound. Maybe I could relax after all.

Chapter Eighteen

When we left home, I thought we were off to work, but Mom turned in a different direction. I liked this new car; I got to be in the front seat next to Mom again. We were in the car for much longer than usual, and I was half fearful and half excited. My nose was full of different smells. How could I describe them? Green! Cows, sheep, grass, corn, and wheat. I was excited.

Mom pulled up outside a building, and I began to panic as she got out and left me there. Where were we? I put my nose out of the window. I could smell something familiar but different; what was it? Mom was back, driving at a snail's pace; we went under a barrier and onto the grass. We stopped again, and Mom got me out. The familiar smell was strong here. I lay on the grass, sniffing as Mom bustled around. Quack, quack and a mommy duck came waddling by with her little ones. The ducklings were quacking away as they followed Mom towards the lake. They were so close I could have bopped one, but I didn't. I just watched this waddling line of cute fluffy ducklings following their mom. I've got it! That's what I could smell! Boppies like in the pet shop! I sniffed and looked around; I needed to find the boppies!

Joey was whining. Why, I wondered? He had settled down quite nicely and taken no notice of the ducklings other than to watch their progress as they waddled past him. Maybe he wanted a walk.

Walking on a lead was still a tricky affair. Joey followed his nose with the occasional moments walking at heel if the mood took him: even that could be trepidatious if he caught the scent of something. He enjoyed standing and sniffing the air, then his nose would go down, and we were off in a zigzag pattern as he followed the scent. He then tended to come to an abrupt stop. As I usually kept pace with him, I often had to take a quick step to the side or over him. Walking at heel, it could be worse. I'd relax thinking, this is nice when he would take off at 90', taking my legs from under me. Occasionally, I ended up flat on the floor with Joey giving me a scornful look, almost like I was disgracing him. I did find, though, that when we did the home walks, because he knew the route we were taking, he began to walk more reliably; it was only away from home that the frantic zigzag and 90' dives came into play. Slowly but surely, we were getting there.

Mom was okay, I decided. If only she would let me off the lead and allow me to find the boppies. She had told me they were called rabbits, but I preferred to call them boppies. Of course, I might find other exciting smells to follow, and who knows where that could lead me? She really hadn't gotten the hang of this walking on a lead lark, though. She sometimes used cuss words when I dived off to follow a scent. I needed to train her properly, and let me take the lead on my lead!

Our first bedtime came. I left Joey out on the secured lead as I pulled out the seat in the back to make a wider bed. It was about the size of a good single bed, enough for us. There was a little hinged piece that you popped out at the end of it to give another six inches in length. I was left with a four-foot by two-foot space on the floor beside the bed. I had pre-rolled my quilt and mattress cover at home to make life easier. I was laying it out so my pillow was at the back of the Berlingo.

Being such a small van, there were compromises like getting undressed and dressed. I couldn't stand up because I had no pop-up top on this van. Everything had to be done sitting down. I figured out I needed to get Joey onto the bed, shut and lock the sliding door, and carefully disrobe without bashing my hands onto the roof. That was the easy bit. Undoing jeans and then lifting your bum a little to wriggle out of them was more challenging. It was all the more difficult when a certain dog decided to come and see what I was doing!

Once that was all achieved, I went to lie down under the quilt. Joey had settled himself, leaning upon my pillow.

"Come on, move." I pointed to the opposite end. Joey blinked.

"Move!" There was no way he would be sleeping on my pillow and snoring in my face.

With a disgruntled sigh, Joey moved down a foot.

"No, down there." I pointed again.

Joey moved to the bottom, and I lay down. That was good. I had room to move my legs around and dangle my feet out if I was hot.

I settled with my book as Joey paced around by my feet, trying to find that perfect spot to curl up. He trampled over me to the edge of the bed and looked down. Out of the corner of my eye, I saw him freeze. He could not take his eyes off the black space beside the bed. I managed to sit up and give him a reassuring cuddle. Quick as a flash, he shot to my pillow and curled up. Cheeky monkey! There was only one thing for it. I grabbed my pillow from under him and turned myself around. I had to sleep tonight with my head at the bottom end of the quilt: the plastic poppers of the cover catching my face all night. Tomorrow, when I got up, I'd change it around.

I was enjoying the camping. Although Mom took up too much of the bed because it wasn't as big as the one at home, we managed okay once I had uncurled myself and pushed her across a bit.

Morning came, and it was cloudy and drizzly. Thankfully, having put the tent up, we had space to sit comfortably. I dressed and opened the door with a reverse procedure from the night before.

After a walk around the site and chats with others doing the same, we got ourselves comfy under the canvas. I was amazed at how well Joey had settled into the camping life. Here I was, sitting outside [ish], enjoying the sounds of nature with the cutest dog curled up on my lap.

Life felt pretty perfect right now. He was relaxed and happy just watching the world around him. I hope he hadn't spotted the rabbits across the site from us. In the early evening, they would quietly slip out of their burrows and hop around the nearby grass.

Boppies! I can see boppies!

My ears came up, my nose twitched, and my eyes scanned the site. But I couldn't see anything moving. Hmm, they must be playing statues. Ah, there's one, woof, woof, woof. I was up and quivering with excitement.

Mom, come on, I want to see the boppies!

I was pulling at my lead but couldn't get further than six feet away. It was very frustrating. But where had the boppies gone? Oh no, my barking must have set them running for their burrows. I must stay quiet next time. With a quick drink of water, I settled back down again to watch. My head was swivelling this way and that, and my nose was on full alert. Mom said something about it being doggie TV.

There was a nice walking path into Winchcombe town from this site, and I decided we would see what it was like. Backpack on with a bottle of water and a bowl for Joey, we set off. It was a nicely mown path, but there was a sign at the start of the path to be mindful of rabbit holes. Carefully, we negotiated our way along the path, with Joey's nose going into every hole and burrow he encountered. It made for a tedious stop-start walk with zigzags. We popped out into the back streets of Winchcombe, and it was quiet. Locals were going from shop to shop and chatting on corners. Everyone seemed to know everyone else. Joey got many admiring looks, and quite a few people stopped to give him a scratch behind his ears. Most people thought he was a girl as he was so pretty. Most people also thought he was a puppy and were very surprised when I said he was ten years old.

He was walking on the lead well and coping with walking around people as we passed them. Thankfully, there were no crowds, as he tends to get missed when there are many people around him, especially since he is so small.

I spotted a small café with a sign outside saying dogs were welcome. I must say, I felt like a cup of tea and a sit-down, but how would Joey react? I walked past and thought, come on, let's see what he's like going into a café. So, we turned around and went back and across the threshold before I could chicken out. Joey headed for the water bowl, and I ordered a cup of tea and an Eccles cake. Joey gathered more fuss from the few people that were in there. I settled for a table in the window, and Joey promptly jumped onto the sofa next to me. Maybe that wasn't such a good idea. I got him off by enticing him with a treat, and he settled under the table, watching the world go by.

It wasn't Joey who put me to shame; he was as good as gold. I put him to shame. The Eccles cake had such flaky pastry that I was dropping crumbs everywhere! Joey had never bothered with human food, so he was entirely at odds with any average dog who would have vacuumed up the crumbs. I apologised to the café owner, who said not to worry at all. She, too, thought it was unusual that Joey had ignored the crumbs.

We took a slow and steady walk back to camp in gentle rain and retreated inside to cook my dinner and feed Joey. As always, I had planned my meals at home and made single portions to go into the fridge. I had a sachet of rice or pasta and some chilli or curry in one pot of boiling water. It worked well. With the lid put back on the pot of hot water once served, I had washing up water, too. Once fed, Joey jumped onto the bench seat to see what was cooking. He seemed to like that he was at nose height to food and could also look out the window to see what was happening. Whilst I ate my dinner, he snuggled down and soon twitched in his sleep, probably chasing rabbits, if I knew anything.

My walking gear was drying out in the tent, and it was too chilly to sit outside after the rain. I stretched out on the seat and soon had Joey curled up on my lap as I read my book. As the sun went down, we stayed happily snuggled up.

Chapter Nineteen

The following morning, there was brilliant sunshine, but Joey had had a restless night. He kept nibbling at his paw, and I couldn't see why. We had a short walk around the site before he had breakfast. Once he had eaten, the paw nibbling began again. I sat down next to him, but I got a little growl every time I went near him. What I could see was that the skin between his pads was inflamed. He must have something stuck there: time to call the vet.

Within minutes of the call, I had leapt into action; they could see him within the hour. The electric cable was swiftly unplugged and thrown inside. Gas turned off, and mugs, plates and dog bowls were thrown into the sink. The toilet emptied, and the tent was pulled down and hurled into the back; another job for later. I took a quick look at my watch; we had forty minutes to get to the vet. It was cutting it fine, but we could do it.

"Joey Moore, please."

It was my favourite vet, Tim. Joey loved him, too, as he gave him lots of cuddles.

"So, what have you done here, young man?"

What are you doing? Why are we here? I can fix this annoying itch; I need to bite it, and it'll be sorted. Oh no, you don't; you're not seeing my paw; it's mine. I snarled to tell him to sod off. Hmm, he's back to stroking me again. See, I told you I could sort it. Right, gimme my paw; I need to nibble.

Hang on a minute; where's Tasha, the nurse, taking me? I only want to nibble a bit; I'm fine, honestly! Bugger, bugger, bugger, I'm in a crate.

Oh my, I'm tired. I'll take a nap, then get back to my paw.

Putting in all my effort, I open my eyes. Bugger, I am still in the crate. Feeling very woozy, I look around to see what is happening. Hang on a minute, there's a blue thing in my crate! What the hell is that? I growl and try to move away, but it keeps following me! I move again, but it is still coming towards me. MOM, what is it?

"Come on, Joey. It's okay; it's just your bandage," Tasha said as she opened the crate. "Let's go and see Tim."

She picked me up and cuddled me. I heard her mention Mom. Thank heavens for that. She'll sort this blue thing out.

"Hello, Joey boy. Look at you with your blue bandage!" I reached out to fuss him as Tasha put him on the examination bench. He looked very sorry for himself.

Get this bloody thing off me; I can't get to my paw! I gave Mom the puppy dog eyes, which always worked. But she took no notice. She was fussing me and talking to Tim. Hmmph. It was Tim's fault I had the blue thing; I didn't like him anymore. No. You can offer me a treat all you like but I'm not having it. No way! This blue thing is around my leg and paw, and it's your fault.

Oh no, what is this thing now? Then I knew. I'd had one of these on before when I had my boy bits taken away: I had loved those licky bits. It was called the cone of shame and was going around my neck. Tim, why can't you wear it instead? You deserve to suffer after what you've done!

With his cone on and antibiotics in my pocket, we headed to the car. Joey quickly adapted to the bandaged leg, but the cone of shame was banged against door frames and people's legs on the way out. Tim had shown me the problem: a centimetre-long grass seed had pierced his skin and, with Joey trying to remove it, had gone further inside. It had been the right call to get him into the vet quickly.

Get this bloody thing off my neck! I can't get to my paw! Actually, my paw was no longer hurting, but I didn't like the blue thing. I jumped up onto the sofa and got thrown backwards as the cone hit the cushion and sent me flying. Mom picked me up instead, but have you ever tried sleeping with your head on rigid plastic when you want to be on a snuggly, fluffy cushion? It wasn't funny at all.

Irritated by the cone, Joey managed to get comfy and sleep. I didn't risk letting him climb the stairs to bed; I carried him instead. I was just so glad to have him back home. I had been worried sick.

I took the next day off work so that Joey could adjust

to the cone. Bosh, into doors, bang, up against walls, scrape, as he went down the steps to the garden and as for eating, that was a whole new thing altogether. Every time Joey approached his bowl, the cone caught on the bottom and stopped his head from getting to it. By the time he had worked out how to negotiate the cone and the bowl, food was all over the kitchen floor, but at least it was easier for him to eat. Drinking was another matter. The cone managed to get caught under the bowl and flip it up; the kitchen was awash, and Joey was disgusted. The cone must come off for meal times to save our sanity.

The cone is off, the cone is off, the cone is off, yeah! Mom had picked me up and took my cone off so we could cuddle. It was so much nicer. I could feel soft cushions; it was bliss. Mom scratched me around where the collar had been: oh, that felt good, I thought as I fell asleep.

Come on, Joey, time for walkies, I heard Mom say. I blinked. How had that collar gotten back on again? MOM! I heard my lead being rattled and jumped off the sofa. I was impressed with myself. I'd done it quite elegantly without crumbling into a cone heap. Lead on and we were off out the door.

There's Bruno! "Hiya, mate."

"Ha, ha, ha, you got the cone of shame!"

"Give over Bruno, like you've never had to wear one!"

"Not for ages, no. With all that fluff splayed out around the cone, you look more like Shakespeare now than ever."

"Sod off, Bruno, or I'll tell that Chihuahua you like that you had a girly pink bandage."

"Okay, it was only a joke. Gotta go, mate."

Within a few days, the cone was off. I breathed a sigh of relief. I had marks on all the paintwork where the cone had argued with the walls. Another few days later, it was back at the vet to get the bandage removed. Thankfully, Joey didn't nibble at the bandage, but he was so happy when it was removed for good!

That ended a camping weekend I didn't want to happen again!

Chapter Twenty

Now that Joey was friendly with the neighbour's dogs, we often went to theirs for a glass of wine and a chat. Whether Joey had been for a walk or not, he focused on heading down the garden to do his business. All four dogs would play follow-my-leader, each taking turns as the Pied Piper. It was comical to watch. When one peed up a bush, the others followed suit, except for Pippa, who was the only female; plus, she bossed the boys around.

Pippa, Pudsey, and Bruno were all characters in their own way. When you sat on the sofa, you were game for being snuggled up to by all three, plus Joey. Pippa wasn't so bothered about being on your lap; Pudsey loved it but often got pushed aside by the young gun Bruno. Joey waited until they were settled before claiming his place right next to me or jumping off and going to curl up with Jayne or Carl. He was content, and it was lovely to see.

On summer days, we sat in the back garden and put the world to right while the dogs milled around playing with their toys. Playing tug was Bruno's favourite. But Joey just watched. He never picked up a ball or tried to play fight. It was like he didn't know how. He preferred to sneak over to Carl and get picked up for a cuddle. Carl was rewarded with many licks, something I hated, but Carl didn't mind. He then settled on Carl's lap and went to sleep. In Joey's eyes, it was man time, and he relished it.

After much persuasion one day, we managed to get Joey to take notice of a ball. The only ball he had at home was one I had unearthed out of the hedge when I first moved there. This half-rotten, punctured leather 'skill' ball should have gone straight into the bin. A skill ball is one-third to half the size of a standard soccer ball. It got thrown to one side and gradually got cleaner as the weather washed it, and because Joey seemed to like it, it never found its way to the bin!

When Joey arrived, it was the one thing he did play with. He pounced on it and then killed it by shaking it in his mouth before running up and down with it and trying to bark simultaneously. And eventually, we played fetch with it once I'd wrestled it from his jaws. I bought a new one because he seemed to love it so much. That got utterly ignored until I purposely punctured and deformed it, and then the same games ensued with added peeling off the coloured layer of coating. But he always preferred the old battered one.

Tennis balls and other throwing and tugging toys were never successful. He didn't know what to do with them, and they became trip hazards in the lounge. I added soft, squeaky toys to his toy box. The toy box was occasionally delved into until he found the right one, and the toy would come out and be attacked.

Ears were ripped off teddy bears, tails ripped off monkeys, and the innards ripped out. Sometimes, he left the lounge looking like snow had fallen indoors with all the stuffing spread around. He wasn't happy until he had pulled the squeaker out of the middle. The stuffing was removed, and he would shred the rest. He would look up at you with bits of fur and threads hanging from his mouth. Any attempt to remove these was met with a quick scoot out the door and away down the garden. He did not give up toys or anything connected to them with ease. Bargaining nearly always had to be done, which meant treats in exchange for wet, disgusting fur pieces.

Round at the neighbours, we decided to see if he would copy Bruno, Pudsey and Pippa and play fetch. We rolled a ball towards him. He stood and watched this thing approach; it stopped when it hit his paws, and he looked up, completely puzzled as to why this thing was there. Then Bruno pounced upon it and ran off with it before dropping it back at the feet of the nearest person. We did this for quite some time with one or other of the dogs running for the ball, and then all three Borders would bark and chase it. Joey continued to watch.

Carl called me over and showed me one of the round things; he said it was called a ball. Yeah, and? He rolled it forward and pointed to it, saying fetch. I blinked and stayed where I was. He tried again. I stretched and lay down.

The three Borders came back up to us and were joyfully

tossing their balls around. Maybe I'll give it a go, so I pinched one of theirs.

Now what? I let it go and nosed it. It didn't smell that good: someone had peed on it. It had an unpleasant texture as it wasn't for eating. I nosed it away, and one of the Borders pounced on it. I shook my head. How can this ball thing make them so happy? I didn't get it.

In a moment of terrier calmness, we rolled the ball again at Joey. His nose came down, and he sniffed. He looked up and into each of our eyes. Head down, he sniffed again. Then his nose nudged it. He still didn't move as it rolled away. We rolled it to him again.

Look down.

Sniff.

Nudge.

On about the fourth attempt, he picked it up, decided he wasn't keen, dropped it, and then peed on it. There endeth any effort to get him to play ball.

Chapter Twenty-One

Life was cushy. I got fed well, got cuddles and had some good friends in my dog possie. Plus, people seemed to love me and always said I was pretty. I'm not sure pretty is the right word for a mature male dog, but I accepted it and enjoyed the fuss.

I loved being around children. They would sit by me for ages, gently stroking my head: I was in heaven.

I enjoyed being with Mom, and although thoughts of my dad were not at the front of my mind these days, I felt happy when I thought about him.

Chapter Twenty-Two

Joey had developed into a solid routine by now. His body clock was finely tuned, unlike mine.

He was awake at 7 am on the dot.

Downstairs for a pee and for me to make a cup of tea.

We returned to bed, and Joey snoozed while I caught up on social media.

7.45 am, jumped off the bed and moaned at me until I got out, washed and dressed.

8 am, lead on and into the car to go to work.

8.45 am, breakfast at work [me too: toast and a cup of tea].

9.05 am, Joey would sleep until the door opened, and a client or neighbour entered the unit.

1 pm, stands whining at the front door, awaiting Paula to appear and take him for his lunchtime walk.

5 pm nag me that it was time to go home.

As I ran my own business, going home time was variable, but I usually tried to be gone by 6 pm. With Joey nagging me, my productivity would diminish, so I soon gave in.

During the day, Joey often liked to come onto my lap for a cuddle. One day, I sat in my office chair with my feet up and him on my lap. He stood up and, without a second thought, stepped onto my desk and began nosing around the computer and all the odds and sods scattered around. He was cheeky! He then sat down and blinked at me as if to say, that's not very exciting, is it? Get me down, please.

He wanted his dinner as soon as we were home, and only then would I be left in peace.

That was until 10 pm when he went to the top of the stairs and waited for me to go up, too.

Why do humans need alarm clocks? Just get a dog!

I wanted to be near Mom all evening, so rather than curling up on the chair or the other end of the sofa, I snuggled up next to her. I felt safe and protected. Bedtime came, and I curled up in the corner while Mom read. She would turn the light out, and it wasn't long before Mom fell asleep. I wanted to be closer to Mom than this, though. What could I do?

I stood up, crept up the bed, and stopped. Mom was still sleeping. I pawed gently at the duvet and made myself cosy between the pillow and the duvet. Mmm, that was nice, but I couldn't feel Mom next to me. I felt the warmth coming from under the duvet. Should I? I looked at Mom, still sleeping. Gently, I snuffled my head under the duvet and went further down the bed. Ah, there's Mom. I snuggled down with my back leaning against hers and went to sleep.

I was feeling hot. I lay in the dark, still half asleep and

realised my back felt strange. I froze, wondering what the heck it was. Gingerly, I moved my hand and felt Joey's little fury body snuggled up against me. Crikey, that had given me a shock! How did I not feel him get into bed? Throwing the duvet aside a little to get some cool air, I soon dozed back off. When morning came, Joey had crept back out of bed and was curled up in the corner again as if he had never moved. Of course, he did it numerous times once he had gotten away with this. Thankfully, not every night!

When I was asleep downstairs, I carefully chose where I wanted to sleep. Mom didn't seem to mind where I was, and I was never told to get off the furniture. I had a nice big bed on the floor but preferred being on the sofa or the chair. Both of those had lovely fluffy cushions. I liked to be comfy! When Mom had her feet up on the sofa, I would lie at the end, leaning uphill on the cushion. It didn't take me long to work out that I could jump across from the sofa to the chair. There was always a gasp on the rare occasion Mom saw me do this, as it was quite a leap, but I knew I could do it.

The only thing was, when I was sitting on the chair, I couldn't see the people walking past. I looked up at the back of the chair; I wondered...I looked at Mom and then back at the chair. Yup, I could do this. With one leap, I was on the top. It was soft and squidgy, but I didn't fall. It was comfy, and from this position, I could watch people walk down the street or come to the door. It was like having live TV! Over a short time, this back cushion moulded into my shape with a nice little dip in the middle. I soon found it was easy to sleep there, too.

One evening, I was napping there and went into a deep sleep. Mom was watching some murder mystery programme, so she was utterly engrossed until she heard a bump. The bump woke me up, as it would do. In my sleep, I had gone to turn and fallen off the back of the chair to the floor. I couldn't let Mom think that was a faux pas, so I stretched tall and casually wandered around the back of the chair to see Mom looking at me. I blinked. I meant to jump down that way, Mom, honest. A little dazed and confused, I was otherwise okay. I went to Mom for a fuss and then hopped back onto the chair and the fluffy cushion, thinking I had better stay safe for the rest of the evening. Doing that a second time would be very embarrassing!

Chapter Twenty-Three

I was getting used to this camping lark and found it fun. I made new friends and had so many new peemails to read when we went for walks that my senses were on overload. Everyone we met said I was cute and looked like a puppy. Everyone loves me!

We arrived at Kingsbury Water Park in the Midlands. It wasn't a considerable distance from home, but enough for me to have a nice nap on the way. Why did I ever worry about travelling in the car? It was warm and cosy, and I had Mom there. I love it now.

A nice man [he gave me a fuss] told us where to park, and Mom quickly had the tent up. She put the bucket loo in the corner and got out her big red chair. I loved this chair. It was big and round and comfy. Mom went inside the van to put the kettle on. I looked around, but she couldn't see me. I checked the length of my lead; there was enough to do what I wanted. I glanced at Mom again; she was still busy, so I did as any dog would: I jumped onto the chair, settled down, and went to sleep. I was dreaming of the lovely little poodle I'd spotted when we came in when I was rudely awoken.

"Joey!"

I ignored it; I was enjoying my dream far too much.

"Joey!"

I raised an eyelid and peered at Mom. She was standing there with a cup of tea, glaring at me.

"Get down off my chair! Your blanket is here." *She said, pointing at the ground.*

I blinked and looked at where she was pointing. Yeah, and? You can sit on it if you like; I don't mind. I shut my eyes again.

"Joey! Move your arse, now!"

With a disgruntled sigh, I figured I had better move; I needed a pee anyway. I jumped off the chair, stretched, and peed up the corner of the awning. I heard Mom mutter some cuss words, but I ignored her. She had woken me up, and I wasn't happy.

We sat outside until darkness had fallen before we went for an evening walk and then bed. Mom nudged me across as usual; she seemed to think I took up a lot of room, but I was only little, and I knew I didn't take up much room at all. Mom read for a bit, and then the light went out. Now, where had I got to in the dream of the pretty poodle?

I loved it here. Kingsbury is over six hundred acres of country park that has fifteen lakes. It's an easy place to spot if you are landing at Birmingham Airport. Different lakes allow different activities, from fishing to water skiing and jet biking. All the ground surrounding the lakes is carefully managed to encourage the wildlife, and you never know what you would see on a quiet walk.

It had been a lovely day, and Joey had been perfectly behaved. It was nice to relax now. I knew he wasn't going to bark like a nutter all the time. Don't get me wrong, he had his moments, but he was playful and happy when he did bark. He was never angry, never snarled or growled. The only bugbear was at bedtime, which was a battle of wills. Getting Joey to stay in his space and not invade mine was a work in progress. With such a small van and no extra space to spread out, we had to work together on the sleeping arrangements. I occasionally woke with him curled near my head. Not a problem until he started snoring!

It was a peaceful, quiet and dark night when I awoke with a start, feeling like somebody was staring at me. With bleary eyes, I looked at my phone. It was 2 am. I mentally went through locking the doors before we got into bed. Knowing I had locked up, I wondered what had startled me. Gingerly, I pulled the top of the quilt down to look around in the dark. A shaft of moonlight was creeping through the curtain by me, highlighting a shadow at the bottom of the bed. Joey was sat bolt upright and had nudged the blackout curtains apart. He was glaring intently outside. Now, I was spooked.

"Joey, what's up, mate?"

Joey took no notice. He was sat perfectly still, staring.

"Joey!"

His head came from around the curtain, and he looked at me.

"What's the matter, boy?"

His head nudged the curtain apart again, and he went back to staring. My heart was racing. I had picked the far side of the site away from others, and no one pitched in shouting distance. That, I realised, could have been a mistake. What if someone had crept on site from the lane behind us and was checking to see what they could steal from the campers? I lay still for a moment, straining my ears for the sounds of someone creeping around or trying the doors, but all I could hear in the distance was owls hooting.

As Joey was still staring intently, there was only one thing for it. Investigate. I put the light on and wriggled into some clothes, which was not easy when the van was so small. I grabbed his lead and unlocked the sliding door. Joey jumped out before me and was pulling at the lead. I grabbed the torch and switched it on. I hoped it wasn't someone trying to get into the vans on site. I shone the torchlight around but could see no one. The only light came from the toilet block nearby. Joey was pulling away from the van and in the direction of the trees lining the lane. I hadn't stopped to slip any shoes on, so my feet were soon soaked with the night-time dew as we searched for whatever had interested Joey.

Casting the beam left and right, Joey stopped. I cast the beam again, and there, about one hundred yards away, sat a bunny. I sighed, so that was what he was after! I let him sniff around with relief before encouraging him back to bed. Opening the van door, I picked Joey up to get him in and put him onto the bed. The quilt cover now had a lovely paw print pattern all over it. I got in and sat on the bed to wipe my feet off from all the grass I had collected: my toes were freezing, and my towel was full of grass. Joey returned to nosing open the curtain and staring at the bunnies. Now I knew what he was fixated on; I locked up and went back to sleep, leaving Joey glaring into the darkness.

We were both groggy in the morning, but after breakfast, it was time for a walk down to the lakes. Knowing I couldn't trust Joey on recall, I had bought his retractable lead. This would allow him more freedom and give me peace of mind, as long as he didn't trip me up!

It was a lovely area to wander around at any time of year. I popped Joey's harness on and attached the lead. By the time we had got to the lane at the side of the site, Joey was in heaven. Snuffling left, right and centre without tripping me up! His nose was into the bushes; then he would scuttle along after a fluttering leaf, back across to the bush and so on. He had one narrow escape when he worked his way into a bush, so intent was he on what he was scenting that he didn't realise there was a stagnant pond right in front of him. I managed to lock off the lead just in time before he sank into the smelly, black goo at the pond's edge. We [he] must have covered triple the distance by the time we reached the first lake.

That lake was about a ten-minute walk from the site. There was a little car park too, and a café. We stopped, sat on a bench for a few minutes, and watched as people with children or dogs wandered past. Then Joey's ears pricked up, and he was staring.

This extending lead was great! I felt free! I could zip along here and there and even run back again. The only thing I didn't like was when it stopped me with a jolt. There was a 'zppt', then a click as it ran to its full length, so I had to wait for Mom to catch up a bit before I could zoom off again. Running back to Mom, it was a long 'zppt' as it coiled back in ahead of me.

I tried to run into the bushes, but the line went taught with a 'zppt', and I stopped in my tracks. Bugger! We sat down by the lake, and I had a big drink of water. I sat there, nose in the air, sniffing the breeze. There were so many smells; it was glorious. I cast my eyes around, watching a young couple walking with a pushchair and an obedient cocker spaniel. Well, that was an oxymoron: when do you see a well-behaved Cocker Spaniel? It must have been for treats! Little dogs were running around, yapping and having fun, a big retriever was slobbering over a tennis ball, and then I saw a man. He was an old man with a walking stick, and I heard a small girl call him Gramps. When I was with Dad, we had two little children visit, and they called my dad Gramps. Could that be my Gramps? It must be Dad. I quivered.

The man was approaching us. My tail started twitching, the wags got bigger, and I stood up. I was trembling in anticipation. But as he got nearer, my twitching nose didn't scent Dad. It was a different man the girls were calling Gramps. He came and sat down on the same bench. It was a shame it wasn't Dad, but I was happy to let him fuss me. I even hopped up on the bench so he could have a cuddle. The children came over, too, and after receiving permission to fuss me, they gently scratched me under my ears. I was in heaven!

Mom liked it when I made people happy; she said it was why I was born, but she made people happy, too.

Joey's reaction to the old man who came to sit with us was strange. I'd witnessed this focused reaction to old men before, and the men always looked very similar. I wondered if he thought they looked like his dad. I wished I knew more about his past life, but that was not to be.

That night, I hoped that Joey would sleep rather than be glaring out the window at the wildlife. We settled down to a peaceful night, or so I thought. I was awoken from a deep sleep by the sound of Joey retching.

"Oh, Joey, what's up?"

I couldn't move as I was pinned under the quilt by Joey, standing up near my head as he retched. Sadly, he hadn't room to jump down on the floor. I was in a bit of a panic. He was going to puke all over the bed. Yuck. I pulled back as much of the quilt as possible before Joey managed to gush forth whatever was annoying him!

His sick was all over my sheet, and now he had stopped retching, he had gone back to the bottom of the bed. Although I could now move, I was stuck behind a load of sick. Other than getting out of the driver's side door completely naked, I couldn't clean up without making body contact with the pile of sick that was quickly soaking into my sheet. I managed to reach across for the tea towel to mop up the sick but was now stuck on how to clean everything up in the middle of the night.

On my knees, I shuffled across to the sink to wet the

tea towel. I wiped the sheet before folding a bath towel over on the area, which was the best I could do at 3 am. Thankfully, Joey was all right, but we took an unscheduled trip to the supermarket the following morning for new bedding and towels!

Chapter Twenty-Four

Life with Mom was a nice, settled routine. We went to work, and I got spoiled by anyone who came in, as they often brought in treats for me. At home, I curled up on the sofa of an evening, occasionally nudging up to Mom for a snuggle. At weekends, we pottered around the house with a visit next door for a chat. Jayne and Carl often had Mom and me around for a few hours so Mom wouldn't get lonely. They were good friends.

Every so often, I went on holiday to stay with Lisa and Nicky. Staying there, too, was fun as I had many other dog friends to play with. We often got muddy on our forest walks, and we had to have a shower when we got back; it did make me look like a drowned rat, though, until I was dry and all fluffed up again. I just hated the smell when I was clean! It was so girly. I rubbed up and down the carpet and the sofa to get rid of the girly scent and get my smell back. Boys should smell like boys and not Crufts champions! On some weekends, we would go camping for a few nights. I loved that. It was time for new smells and new people to fawn over me and other dogs to have a chat with. Life was better than I ever thought it could be after I got taken from Dad.

It looked like we were off camping again, as Mom was packing the Berlingo with bags. Bags of clothes, bags full of my food and spare blankets. Much more stuff was being packed than when we usually went camping: what was she up to? When she had finished, we went for a nice walk before getting into the car.

"We are going on holiday, Joey. We are going to Cornwall to see Gill!"

Joey cocked his head to one side, listening.

"I know she is going to spoil you rotten."

We set off on the four-hour drive, and, as expected, Joey was in barking mode. Thankfully, he settled down and slept once we got onto the motorway. It was going to be a long drive. It was the longest I had ever done, where I had to do all the driving and not split it with someone else. The journey was uneventful, thankfully. We stopped after a few hours to give us both time to stretch our legs. Going on a long trip had quietened Joey down while travelling. That was a result.

I'd never met Gill in person, but we were friends in the same Facebook group and regularly talked on the phone. It would be nice to spend a week in the company of someone different and interesting.

I had rented a house at Hannafore in Looe, and Gill

arranged to meet me just outside the area and show me the way. Joey had done well on the journey, with just one short break. By the time we were getting close to our destination, I was feeling tired.

We had stopped! I woke up and stretched from the tip of my tail to my nose; this always gave me an involuntary shudder of pleasure. My lead was clipped on, and I jumped out. Fresh air! We trotted across the car park towards a lovely, smiley lady sitting on a bench. As soon as she spoke, I recognised her voice from Mom's phone calls; it was Gill! I jumped straight on her lap to give her lots of kisses. I knew this lady was lovely, and I wouldn't move from her lap until I had to!

It was lovely to finally meet Gill in person, and she was as lovely as I thought she would be; Joey was definitely taken with her as he followed her everywhere. After such a long journey, I looked forward to settling into our holiday home for the week. After a short walk and a cup of tea, we followed Gill down the lanes and into Looe, over the bridge, and down to Hannafore.

The cottage I had rented was huge. It had five bedrooms, two lounges, a vast kitchen and a boot room. Why so big for one person and a dog, you ask? It was the only one I could get in the available area. Gill helped me unload everything, with Joey trailing her backwards and forwards before she left us to settle in. She had brought me a Cornish Pasty for my tea, and I was salivating at the thought of eating it. I don't care what anyone says; no other pasty is as good as a proper Cornish one.

It was my turn for the twitching nose: I could smell plug-in air fresheners. I hated those things as they gave me a dry throat and a cough: some chemicals in them, namely formaldehyde, benzene, and phthalates, are not good for your health. I systematically went around the house, turning the darned things off, and began to wheeze as I did so: I needed my inhaler. I made a mental note to either turn them back on as I left at the week's end or leave a note saying they were off.

Knowing Joey would not keep off the furniture, I had brought several blankets to cover the sofas and one for the bed. Trying to get him to understand he wasn't allowed up was a lost cause, but covering things up was a simple solution. I shut off the rooms I didn't think I'd use and settled into the remaining space. The first thing Joey did? Yup, you've got it, jumped straight up onto the sofa. It was his ideal perch to people-watch as the lounge window was huge: it must have been about ten feet wide!

Oh, this was good. I was slightly higher than the road on my settee, and it was cosy on these new blankets. I had a whole settee to myself as Mom sat on another one with her feet up. That sofa was weird, as the bottom bit stretched out at the touch of a button, and it raised her feet. How cool was that? I pondered about going into the space underneath, but I was far too happy looking at the people and dogs walking by to give it more thought. I wondered what smells were out there. Surely it was walkies time?

I pestered Mom until she relented; yeah, walkies. We headed down the path and through the gate and turned right. Mom had put my coat on as there was a fine drizzle, but I didn't care; I just wanted to explore. I sniffed the air... it was different to home. It was salty. We went down a few paths, and the salty smell got stronger. We were at the sea!

I was not sure if Joey had been to the seaside before. It can be frustrating not knowing an adopted dog's background sometimes. But I wondered how he would react on the beach. The weather was truly awful. It was certainly what I would call 'Cornish mizzle'. Mizzle is a Cornish/Devon term encompassing many weather conditions. Usually, it is extremely fine light rain and mist or fog that soaks you in minutes. It is never pleasant!

The tide was in, but there was a small area of beach we could walk on safely. Joey trotted down the steps quite happily, his nose fixed on the ground. No stone, piece of seaweed or debris was left without being investigated. So many new smells for him. It was with some surprise to him that his feet suddenly got wet. He looked disgusted at the waves that had washed around his paws and hopped back onto the sand. He was not impressed. Then it happened again, and I could see him trying to work out why it was happening. He didn't mind walking through puddles, but seawater seemed to be a different thing altogether.

Even on that brief walk, we were drenched, and by the time we got back to the holiday home, we needed a good towelling off before putting our feet up. It had been a long day for both of us, and an evening in front of the TV was what we needed.

The homeowner had left many details about the area and the WIFI password, but I needed help to get any signal even though it said I was logged in. I had minimal phone coverage, provided I went upstairs and stood on the front bedroom balcony. I messaged Victoria, the home-owner and asked if there was something I should be doing.

Victoria said no, it should be fine. They had it upgraded the previous week as they knew there was a problem. Victoria said she would speak to the installer and pop around in the morning. I thanked her and said I'd appreciate it if it was no trouble. I left it at that, as I didn't want to fiddle with something I knew nothing about.

The following day was bright and sunny, and true to her word, Victoria appeared at 10 am. Joey alerted me from his position on the arm of the sofa. Remember the no dogs on furniture rule? Damn, I meant to ensure he wasn't on there when Victoria came. I bet I was in for a telling-off!

With introductions made, she came into the lounge. Letting go of Joey, he jumped straight onto the sofa nearest Victoria to get a fuss off her.

"Oh, I'm sorry, that's why I've covered the sofas."

"Oh, don't worry, I've already seen him on there."

"You have?" I was puzzled.

Victoria laughed, "Yes, I only live next door, so I've seen him watching the world go by. I don't have a problem as he is well-behaved, and you have taken precautions." She smiled.

"Thank you. I appreciate it."

"Now, let me look at this receiver thing."

Victoria went to the booster box in the corner socket, closely followed by her new best friend, Joey.

"I spoke to my chap and had plugged in the wrong thing. The WIFI comes from our house, and the booster should be plugged in here."

With a pull-out and a push-in, the booster began flashing red and then settled green.

"Okay, try that."

I flipped on my phone's WIFI and picked it up immediately.

"Yeah, brilliant, I've got a strong signal. Thank you for sorting that out."

"No problem. Is there anything else?"

Joey was now eliciting fuss again.

"No, we're fine, thanks."

She left us to it with a smile, but I was still cringing about her seeing Joey on the furniture!

In between the mizzle, we had some bright and sunny days, which was delightful for late October. It was a pleasure to have the small Juliet balcony in the bedroom. The sun poured in, and the view out to sea was enchanting. With the sun on the front of the house and a paved garden area, I could understand why the patio furniture was out the front; it was a sun trap.

Checking the front garden gate was shut, I opened the front door and, carrying my laptop, went out to the patio table in the sunshine to do some writing. Joey spent quite some time exploring the garden and determining the best place to sit. He seemed torn between being right by the gate in the shade or leaning up against the house wall in the sunshine. The latter won, meaning he could enjoy the warmth and still see anyone walking by. He could quickly run to the gate if he thought there was a chance of saying hello to another dog or a human.

His ears pricked up at the sound of a car approaching. His tail began to wag, and he ran to the gate: it was Gill. No sooner had she set foot in the garden than she was smothered in doggy kisses.

Chapter Twenty-Five

Gill is a gem of a friend. She had been at work all morning but insisted on making us a cup of tea and bringing it back out to enjoy the sunshine. Joey was like Velcro; he would not leave her side! Wherever Gill went, Joey followed. We sat and enjoyed the sun's warmth, with Joey trying to climb on her lap. He was nothing but a trier, was this dog. It was so funny to see after us being just me and him for so long. He gave up eventually and lay by her feet, regularly looking up to ensure she had not disappeared.

Gill was stopping over that night, and she had checked out that the local hotel allowed dogs into the bar and dining area. They had no problem with it, so we happily walked to the hotel for our evening meal. As expected, out of season, it was deserted except for a few people sitting at the other end of the room. We settled at a corner table. I had no idea how well Joey was going to behave, but once he had surfed the floor for any stray titbits, he lay down and went to sleep; he was full of surprises. I was getting the feeling that he was the perfect 'pub dog'. Shame I rarely went to pubs! With his immaculate behaviour, I saved some of my fish so he could have a nice treat when we returned to the holiday home. From being very nervous about this holiday and Joey's reactions, I was pleasantly surprised at how well-behaved he could be.

Now that the rain had stopped, it was an enjoyable stroll back to the house. Once through the door, Joey began nuzzling at my pocket for his treat. I unwrapped his fish titbits and dropped them into his bowl. He snuffled contentedly for mere seconds as they were devoured. Anyone would think he was never fed!

Once his treat was eaten, he leapt onto Gill's lap. He sat there proud as punch with his new best friend before turning around and lying across her. Poor Gill couldn't move! Thankfully, he didn't try to follow her into her bedroom when we went to bed!

It was morning at last. Mom had to lift me onto the bed as it was so high, so I never got down to mooch around; otherwise, I wouldn't have been able to get back up. But now it was light, and I wanted to see Gill again; I knew she was in another room, so I snuck out the door while Mom was dozing. On the landing, my senses told me which room Gill was in. I pushed at the bedroom door and bounded onto the bed; Gill needed morning kisses! Thankfully, she enjoyed them, and the sound of Gill laughing woke Mom. I'd made her happy! Mom put her head around the door; oops, I gave her my most appealing smile and wagged my tail.

"Come on you, leave Gill alone. Time you went outside anyway."

I jumped off the bed and headed downstairs. Now Mom had mentioned going out, I was bursting. But can I have breakfast next, please, Mom?

I was surprised when I entered the lounge: a big helium birthday balloon and a bag of gifts! I hadn't realised that when Gill had popped out to the car as we went to bed, she had secretly brought these in for my birthday! It was such a lovely surprise. But Joey was growling. I could not work out why. He was hiding behind the sofa and peeking out to growl towards the TV. It was then I realised that he was growling at the balloon! The balloon was moving with the draft generated from us moving around, and he thought we were in imminent danger. Thankfully, we found a place where it didn't waft around at the slightest draft, and the growling stopped. He was a silly boy! Meanwhile, I tucked into the retro sweets Gill gave me for my birthday: a very thoughtful gift.

Today, we were off to Looe for a walk around and lunch. It was such a beautiful day that we were in short-sleeved tops. On the way there, Joey insisted on sitting on my lap, which was a blooming pain as he wouldn't sit still! I was scratched here, there, and everywhere! We parked up, and no sooner had we got out of the car than Joey was engulfed in cuddles by a lady doing her shopping.

"Oh, what a gorgeous puppy; what's his name?"

"Joey, he's ten years old."

"Ten? My oh my, he looks like he's a puppy! Border Collie?"

"No, he's a Sheltie/Cocker cross."

"Oh, he is gorgeous. Cynthia, come here and see this lovely dog; how old do you think he is?"

"Oh, you're a lovely girl," Cynthia said as she bent down to fuss Joey. "Ooh, I don't know, about two?"

"No, he's ten, and it's a boy; he is so pretty."

After another cuddle and receiving licks of adoration from Joey, they wandered up the high street, still talking about how lovely he was.

I was enjoying the attention I was getting. It made walking through all the legs of people far more enjoyable. The problem with being small is that people don't always see you; it can be pretty frightening. Thankfully, Mom ensured we were given enough space to walk without me getting knocked or trodden on.

Ooh, a nice smell. I dived in front of a pair of legs to get to a drain pipe.

"Joey!"

I'd almost pulled Mom over in my haste, causing the man I darted in front of to stop abruptly. I could hear Mom apologising on my behalf.

There were lots of dogs around, too. Some were nice, friendly ones, but I growled right back when one growled at me. I didn't care what size he was; he wouldn't get the better of me! The only thing was, it scared Mom when I reacted like this, as she didn't like me having a go at other dogs. It was not so bad if they were aggressive first, but I was in trouble if I started it. Little did she realise that I was scared stiff of some dogs. There had been instances in my past where I had been bullied and had to fight my corner. That was why I was so snappy at puppy dog training; I needed to assert myself.

Walking up the street with Joey wasn't too bad. More people smiled at Joey and stopped for a fuss. Some dogs ignored him, others wanted to attack him, and with macho pride at stake, he wanted to have a go, too, on occasions. But in general, we were okay.

I was a small child when I last visited Looe with my parents, two older brothers, and our Pembroke Corgi, Lass. Looe is a lovely place that has retained much of its old-world charm and is still a working fishing port. You could smell the fish brought in that morning by walking along the harbour. The trawlermen were busy unloading the crates of catch into their business area, ready to be prepared for sale. Many had blackboards out the front displaying the day's catch for sale to the public. There was a wide variety from monkfish to lemon sole and the common mackerel: mackerel seemed to jump from the water into the boat around the British coast! Like any trawler fishing port, it was a delight to the taste buds if you were a fish lover.

On the harbour wall, children were dangling crab lines. Plastic buckets beside them were half full of seawater in anticipation of catching something. They are proud to show off their catch to everyone. I remember doing the same when I was little, too: making memories that last forever. A few fishermen cast their rods from the wall and into the sea. The most common thing they pulled in was whiting or dogfish. Now we were in the colder months, mackerel was less of an option. But I'm not sure whether catching a fishy supper was what they were after. I had a sneaky suspicion that fishing was also about being at one with nature. The crashing of the waves, the salty wind off the sea, and just being absorbed in their pastime. When you saw a line go taut, you watched with anticipation to see what would come from the depths. Sometimes a tiddler, a fish so small it was only good for bait. Or something you could take home for tea would emerge, glistening on the hook in the sunshine.

We wandered around the shops before Gill led us to a pub with a beautiful outside eating area. It had enough shade to keep Joey cool, and a waiter even gave us a bowl of water for Joey. The place was busy with autumn tourists enjoying this unusual spell of lovely weather. All the tables quickly filled, and there was a relaxed buzz of chatter around us. When the waiter arrived with our lunch, we were already salivating at the lovely smells as the staff walked past our table with other orders. We had a gorgeous lunch of whitebait and chips as we sat in the sun, with Joey being the chief taster of whitebait!

Joey had very pleading eyes at the smell of fish and was on his best behaviour. I put a couple to one side to take them home for a treat later, even though he had already sampled a few. Yes, Joey was spoilt!

Joey and I had a lovely holiday despite some days being very wet. Gill was doing her utmost to ensure we had a great time. We appreciated her taking the time after work to show us the sights. Joey and I had lovely walks along the seafront and the coastal path. It was a very bonding experience for us both. I was much more relaxed, and Joey wasn't trying to escape at every opportunity. I still didn't trust him, though!

Gill had invited us to her home to meet her husband, Trevor, and their dog, Jet. I was unsure how this would go as Joey was still fearful of some big dark dogs, and they didn't come much bigger or darker than Jet. Jet was a black Newfoundland.

Gill understood my fears and reassured me that Jet was a gentle giant. When I arrived, he was lounging at the garden gate, so we couldn't get in! Gill managed to rouse him and entice him into the kitchen with a treat. Joey warily came with me into the house, looking left and right.

I'd seen the big back dog, but where had he gone?

I looked around. I could smell a dog; there was evidence of a dog, but where was he? One gentle step at a time, I went into the lounge. Stay close to Mom, I thought; she will protect me. There was a smiley man on the settee who called me over. With one last look around, I approached his hand, sniffed, and let him fuss me. Oh, he was a nice man; I wagged my tail. He liked me, so I can do this...

"Joey! Get off!"

But Mom, I've only jumped on the sofa like I do at home!

I ignored Mom as the man was fussing me again. It was his settee, and if he said it was okay, then I was staying here. Mom sat down near me, and I felt comfy and safe.

Joey settled quite happily on the settee next to Trevor and absorbed all the fuss he could get.

"Okay, I'll bring Jet in slowly," said Gill.

"I'll keep Joey on his lead as I don't know if he will lunge or hide!"

I was feeling as nervous as Joey felt!

The door reopened, and in came Jet. Never have I known such a beautiful, docile dog. Being a Newfoundland, he was a big lad typical of his breed. Joey was still busy getting cuddles off Trevor, so he hadn't noticed Jet appear. I called his name, and he turned his head.

"Joey, who's this?"

I was enjoying my cuddles when Mom called my name. I turned my head, and out of the corner of my eye, I saw this big black shape lumber into the room. Jesus! Was it a bear? It must be a bear; he was huge! I didn't know what to do. Should I fight him? No, he's way too big. Should I growl? No, he is definitely way too huge!

What should I do?

I looked at Mom, back at the bear, and then decided. I would hide behind Mom until the bear went away. In a few steps, I scarpered from Trevor's lap to Mom and sat there trembling. I realised I didn't like bears!

Joey started to calm down again, and Jet looked utterly puzzled as to why this little dog was shaking. He had no idea that Joey was frightened of him. Joey poked his nose under my arm to see Jet, who had his nose on my lap. Tentatively, he moved his head a little further forward and sniffed. Jet opened his mouth and lolled out his tongue, and Joey shot his head back behind me again, which is where he stayed for the length of our visit! Jet, the poor lad, was led away into the kitchen so we didn't stress Joey out further.

Although it wasn't the best experience in Joey's life, it did prove to be another bonding experience for the two of us. His trust in me had increased.

After Joey and I explored more of the area on foot, Gill suggested we take a trip to Polperro the next day. I hadn't been there for many years, so it would be nice to go back and see what had changed if anything.

Polperro is a traditional Cornish fishing village of just under six hundred people, which is very small indeed. It is very much one road in and the same road out. During the height of the tourist season, it is crammed with people flip-flopping down the hill to the harbour. All laden with bags, buckets and spades, lilos and deckchairs. At this time of year, it was still popular, but everyone was wrapped up in winter jackets to protect them from the wind. We parked in the car park at the top of the hill and began the walk down to the harbour.

Everything seemed the same as it did when I was a child. Lots of tourist shops selling candy floss and rock with Polperro written through the middle. Beach balls of all sizes hung from the front canopy in vibrant reds, oranges and yellows. Windmills stuck into buckets of sand, whizzing around as the wind caught them. Snorkels and fins from tiny children's sizes to adults. Some things don't change.

The beautiful cottages at the side of the road retained their charm. But I was saddened to see that most were now holiday lets. I couldn't help but feel that the spirit must die for this lovely little place when the holiday season was over. Undoubtedly, the locals couldn't afford to buy the cottages to live in. In most parts of Cornwall, jobs were seasonal and poorly paid, so the majority weren't in a position to get a mortgage on these lovely little places. That made me sad.

We wandered past several craft shops, pottery being one of the more common options down here, along with the jeweller shops and galleries showcasing local artists' work. The Cornish light and the golden beaches are famous worldwide for artists, especially the Newlyn School of Art, developed in the 1880s. Polperro had an old-world charm about it, and with such a small harbour area, it was a beautiful location to capture the view, the weather and the people.

Many tales were told of smugglers in the 18th and 19th centuries, which is probably why so many pubs were called The Smugglers. Goods were brought in at night and hidden in the cliffs or houses near the harbours, awaiting distribution to the locals and merchants who sold them further afield. It was a way of survival in those days, and you could feel that history as we walked down the hill.

It was a shame that when we got to the harbour, it didn't appear anywhere was open for lunch. Gill and I had thought we could get a nice bar meal or a ploughman's lunch down here, but it seemed we were out of luck. We did find one pub open that said it was doing food and allowed dogs inside. I lifted the latch on the door and stepped in. It was gloomy. At the bar stood three men who stopped chatting as soon as the door opened: I hate that! I looked back at Gill before going any further. At a glance, as I turned, I noticed something on a table to my right. I stared at it for a moment.

"Let's go, Gill. It's too dark in here." Thankfully, Gill didn't argue.

We hurried back outside.

"What's up?" asked Gill.

"There were mouse droppings on the table!"

"Oh bugger, let's go and find somewhere once we've got back to the car."

We had driven almost back to Looe when Gill said, "I know," and veered off to a left-hand lane into the countryside. A few minutes later, we arrived at The Coddy Shack.

"This'll fill us up nicely after that walking."

"Great, do they allow dogs?"

"Of course, just round the back in the covered bit."

I followed Gill through the restaurant and out to the back area, which was a large marquee. Perfect. We sat down and relaxed, awaiting our fish and chips. I think I ate fish every day whilst I was away. It was a generous portion of fish, that's for sure. It hung over the edges of the plate! "Plenty of leftovers for you, Joey."

The last few days of the holiday went well, and Joey was as good as gold. I said goodbye to Gill, as did Joey, with lots of licks, and we set off back to the Midlands. On the journey back home, Joey got into the car and lay down, and I hardly heard a peep out of him. Now, that was certainly less stressful for me driving!

It wasn't until the next day that I realised I had left something behind. Gil had greeted me with a bag of goodies: sweets and biscuits. With the vast kitchen in the holiday home, I had left most things on the work surface, but I had put the treats in the cupboard for some reason. I'd completely forgotten them! Ah well, a nice treat for Victoria when she came to inspect the property after I'd left!

Chapter Twenty-Six

That holiday was a real turning point for us. Driving to work was no longer a stress-headache, nerve-tingling forty minutes. Joey even lay down most of the time now. There was no barking, clawing, or mad capers. It was heavenly.

We settled into a nice routine; he was a much calmer dog, and I was a much calmer dog mom. He knew he was onto a good thing where treats were involved and that he was thoroughly spoiled. I could only hope this peace and harmony would continue.

Chapter Twenty-Seven

Adjusting to being single after twenty-four years of marriage was slightly weird. I still shopped as if there were two of us and cooked that way, too. Thank heavens for freezers! I also ended up working crazy long hours. Yes, that's what most people did with their own business, but I was wearing myself out.

The good thing about Joey and I was that we made a great team. We completed each other. I've never been maternal, but having a dog suited my nature and life. I felt complete and happy.

With Joey around, I had someone else to think about, care for, and love. It certainly made me realise that I was not ready to have another man in my life yet. I needed to enjoy being single and have adventures with my boy.

My mental health improved. I was more relaxed, and we enjoyed going out and about for walks in the countryside or camping. I was having fun! I was regaining my confidence in myself, and it seemed like the jigsaw pieces of my life were all falling into a new place, and I liked it. I felt independent and in control for the first time since my divorce. My health improved as I reduced my work hours and adjusted my priorities. If they ever hand out pets on prescription, get a version of Joey!

As Joey had been such a good boy, I bought him a new toy as a treat. It was a giant yellow flattish duck! It was almost as long as he was, with only one squeaky element. I knew it wouldn't take him long to remove the squeak, but I wasn't expecting the response I did get when I gave it to him.

Joey didn't play with toys much. They were there for destruction, just like the ball in the garden. He was not happy until he had pulled them to pieces. His toy box was a sad group of soft toys with missing ears, ripped-open stomachs and things that no longer resembled their original form. Seeing him pull and tear at a cute teddy bear till it was massacred was funny. He would look up gleefully with shining eyes, bits of fluff around his mouth. I'd then have to distract him with a treat so I could do the forensics: collecting up soggy dog toy innards and ripped limbs and deciding what I could repair and what needed more advanced surgery. Of course, some got to the point that they were past their use and were binned.

But this duck. Well, this duck was made of stronger stuff. He didn't seem to want to tear into it; he was very gentle with it. Strange.

I was in the kitchen cooking when I realised it had gone very quiet in the lounge. Strangely quiet.

I crept towards the door and peered in. Joey had his back paws pinning the tail end of the duck down and his front paws cuddling it. Yes, Joey was humping the duck! I shook my head and left him to it. A dog has to do what a dog has to do, and today was hump a stuffed duck day!

Chapter Twenty-Eight

Spurred on by the overall success of our summer holiday in Cornwall, I booked us a Christmas break in the New Forest, Hampshire. I adore the New Forest. I have visited it since I was a very small child, and I have many happy memories of it. When I was there, it made me feel at peace with myself.

The New Forest covers over two hundred square miles of woodland, heathland and grassland. Horses and deer roam freely, and you may come across five different types of deer. Roe, red, fallow, sika and muntjac. The autumn rutting season not only wows you with the spectacular colour of the trees, but you get a chance to watch stags entangling antlers to see who the head of the herd is and who gets the first choice of the females. Walking in the New Forest, I have startled many a roe deer that then skitted off across the ferns and heather and disappeared. Meanwhile, I would be so entranced that my foot would end up in a peat bog and have to be pulled hard to get it out!

The Forest is a haven for bird life, reptiles and fungi. Woodland sections are gated to refuse entry during specific seasons to allow breeding and for the delicate and rare fungi to grow without being picked or trodden on. Wardens drive around, ensuring that these areas are protected at all times. Dotted between the forests are beautiful villages, often linked by walking or cycling paths, Brockenhurst being my favourite.

I couldn't find affordable holiday cottages in my favourite places, so I plumped for one in a small village called Bramshaw. It was not an area I was familiar with, but with only a few hundred occupants, I would have blinked and missed it if I had driven through it. Being in the middle of the forest, it was going to be nice, I was sure.

The car was packed, and Joey was in his harness and seatbelt on the front seat. I packed a bag into the passenger footwell with a blanket on top, just in case I had to make an emergency stop, and he shunted forward. Plus, it gave him some extra space to stretch into on our two-and-a-half-hour drive.

Now that I knew I wasn't returning to that cell, I enjoyed car journeys. We usually went to fun places and met fun people. The adventures were good. Being able to sit in the front seat was cool! I could see so much if I wanted to, and I was next to Mom. I found that comforting. It didn't take long before the warmth and movement sent me to sleep, dreaming of new adventures.

"Whassat?" I woke from sleep as Mom returned to the

car and drove into a courtyard. I could hear the crunch of the gravel underneath the tyres, but there was something else. I shook my head and stretched as I stood up on the seat. Wow, buddies! Running toward us came three dogs. Don't run them over, Mom! Yeah, I had playmates! Mom got out of the car and was immediately surrounded by a Labradoodle, a Golden Retriever, and a Jack Russell. Let me out, Mom, I want to play!

"Wait there one minute, Joey, whilst I get sorted."

After fussing with each wagging dog, I approached the homeowner, Sally, who had emerged from the main farmhouse.

"Hello, you must be Alison; welcome to The Old Dairy. Would you like to get your dog, and I'll show you around?"

We shook hands, "Thank you, won't be a minute."

"Come on, Joey. Let's explore." Joey needed no encouragement to jump out and get himself nose to nose or nose to bum with his new pals.

"Ordinarily, I'd say let him off, but the 'doodle is in season, so better kept on a lead."

"Of course, no problem. He's a bit of a Houdini anyway, so unless I know a place is secure, he stays on his lead."

"Well, the garden for the cottage is secure, so he will be fine there."

She opened the door to the old dairy, "Here you go, perfect for you and Joey, I think."

I unclipped Joey from his lead, and off he went exploring.

Ooh, a new place. I sniffed the air. It smells clean. What's in here? I poked my head around a door. Ah, the loo. There was nothing for me there, then. I turned around and came back into the kitchen. Hmm, there's not much to explore here. What's through the other door? Oh yes, a bed! With one practised leap, I was up. I sniffed, turned around, and lay down.

"Joey! Get off there this minute!" I was embarrassed at his blatant attitude.

"Don't worry; if you have a blanket to cover the bed for him, it's fine."

I'm so sorry, he's a cheeky bugger. Yes, I always carry blankets to cover the furniture. Sorry again."

She chuckled. "No worries, he's a sweet-looking chap; I'm sure he won't be a problem." She walked to the door. "If you need anything, just give us a knock, and we will help if we can. Oh, and some homemade biscuits are in the tin for you."

"That's very kind. Thank you. I'll pop the kettle on while I grab my stuff."

I left Joey in the garden whilst I got our bags from the car. When I returned, he was happily watering fence posts and the owner's three dogs had gone inside. It was a bright and beautiful afternoon for December, so I took advantage of it before the sun died and the air turned chilly: a frost was expected overnight, and I took my cup of tea into the garden. The paddock we overlooked had chicken pens in one corner, and the hens were strutting around happily, scratching at the dirt. The watery sun dipped behind the trees, casting huge dark shadows across the paddock. I noticed Joey was sniffing the air. He was moving towards the fence and sniffing again. What had he caught the smell of?

I looked around. The hens had taken themselves off to bed apart from a couple of slow coaches and I couldn't see anything else: or could I? I let my gaze follow Joey's eye line, and I could see something moving around in the shade of the trees. But I couldn't fathom what it was. The shape was tall and moving towards the edge of the shaded area. Joey was backing away from the fence. As the shape emerged from the shade, he scarpered behind my legs, growling. I could now see why: it was an emu!

Now Joey could see what it was; he was inquisitive and slowly nosed out from between my legs. Gaining confidence with every sniff, he edged towards the fence.

What is that thing? It's way too big to be a chicken. I mean, it's about twenty chickens high. It is as tall as a human on two legs, but I know it isn't human with that long neck, and it's feathery all over its big blob of a body. It has weird, knobbly knees, though. It was coming over to us. Eek, Mom, what do we do? I'm not scared, I'm not afraid... I'm a brave boy; Mom says so. A fence was between us; I was safe, and Mom was safe. What if he comes over the fence at us, though? Mom, I'm scared!

I'll hide behind Mom; I'm sure she can handle it.

"Joey, it's an emu, it's okay." I picked Joey up so he was head height to the emu whose curiosity had him coming towards us. I stood far enough back so that we could all get the measure of each other, and it came up to the fence. Its inquisitive head twitched from left to right as it weighed us up. Its huge eyes blinking at me and then Joey. We stayed still. The emu decided we were not exciting and ambled away. I put Joey back down. "There you go, boy, nothing to worry about." He didn't look convinced. "Come on, let's go inside and get your dinner. I think you have had enough excitement for today."

Chapter Twenty-Nine

The weather was particularly wet and the forest incredibly soggy, so walks were limited to where there was a suitable path. I've been caught too often walking in the forest, and suddenly, my walking boot was submerged in boggy ground. But we went out and about, visiting old haunts from my childhood. I had so many memories of those happy days rushing around in my head.

My favourite place, Mudeford Quay, lies on the coast. When I was a child, this was a sleepy, remote quay with a handful of parking spaces for fishermen, sailors, and tourists. Today, the village has expanded with modern housing, a concrete walkway to Highcliffe, and larger parking areas, but it still retains the beauty I fell in love with as a child.

Christmas day began with low clouds and drizzle. I packed some sandwiches and water to make a cuppa when we arrived, and off we went.

We pulled into the all-too-familiar car park, which was packed. I was feeling despondent as I couldn't find a parking space, but on the second circuit, I spotted someone about to leave and dived into the space. Obviously, I wasn't the only one who fancied a stroll on the beach on Christmas day! The drizzle had eased, and we set off along the prom for our walk.

I sniffed the sea air. There were many fishy smells, and the crab pots smelled great. There were lots of peemails for me to sniff at and respond to. Ooh, hello. Why has that dog got antlers? It was a dog, I'm sure.

"Oy mate, what's with the antlers?"

"Blooming Christmas innit. My Mom thinks I look cute in them. And have you seen the stupid coat I've got on, too?"

I looked along his back. "You're a reindeer and an elf? Jeez, why do moms do it to us? Thank heavens I don't have to wear things like that."

"You're lucky, mate."

With that, he got hurried along by his mom and dad.

Oh, blimey, there was more. Long-suffering dogs dressed as Father Christmas, elves, fairies, and some with tinsel wrapped around their collars-now that must itch!

I didn't expect to see so many people, especially with the grey, wet weather. I was surprised that so many were walking in the drizzle, at picnic benches, and having a light lunch. There was even a family sitting at a bench eating sandwiches and drinking champagne! Now, I wish I had thought of that, but then again, I had to drive, so I wouldn't have been able to drink it anyway. Most people walking along greeted each other with a 'Merry Christmas' and a smile. It was a lovely atmosphere despite the weather.

We were getting rather wet, so I decided to curtail the walk, use the loo, and then head back to the car to dry off. That's where the plan went wrong. Both sets of toilets along the prom were locked shut. Aargh! That wasn't good for all the people who needed to go! Thankfully, I had a plan B.

We got back to the car and got in. I shut all the curtains, locked the doors, and got out my little bucket loo. It was nothing fancy, but I was glad I had brought it. Joey looked at me quizzically, gave up whatever thoughts he had, and then poked his nose around the curtain to see out.

"No, Joey, not for a minute!"

Heaven forbid someone walked past and looked in whilst I was indisposed! How embarrassing would that be?

With the bucket loo secured again, I opened the curtains and dried Joey off while the kettle boiled for a cup of tea. Feeling content, I put my feet up to eat my sandwiches while the dampness from our clothes and fur steamed up the windows. The rain was now lashing down, and I felt pretty smug that we were cosy inside. The car park was emptying rapidly, and I decided to head back to Dairy Cottage before I dozed off.

When we returned, the rain had stopped, and the sun had broken through. To Joey's delight, his three new buddies came out to say hello just as we had gone through the cottage gate. Two poked their heads over the top, and the little one snuffed at the bottom. Joey, meanwhile, went from top to bottom, snuffling and barking. He liked this game.

Sally poked her head out of the door. "Merry Christmas, Alison and Joey!"

"Merry Christmas, Sally," I called back.

"We are having family over this evening, and we would love for you to join us if you wish."

"Oh, that's lovely, if you are sure?"

"Of course, bring Joey; they can all have some fun while we eat. There is only a left-over buffet, but there's plenty to go around, including for the dogs. See you about 7 pm?"

"Great, thank you."

I spent the next hour debating whether we should go or not. It would be rude if we didn't, but did I want to spend time with a large family group I didn't know? I decided to pop over for an hour, have a drink, and then come back. I did have friends and family to call, so that was my excuse to leave early.

With a certain amount of nerves, I knocked on the door. We were welcomed by Sally's son, who shepherded us into a huge country kitchen. The table was laid with leftover cold cuts and salad. People were chatting and nibbling at the food, and the dogs were doing their best begging eyes at the nearest person. It was a lovely cosy environment, and we soon settled in, chatting to Uncle Somebody, whose name I can't remember, with Joey, suitably stuffed on turkey and goose, curled up asleep between us.

Over two hours later, I thanked Sally and returned to the cottage. The TV was on, and we both lay on the bed to watch the Christmas programmes and dozed off. It had been a good day.

Chapter Thirty

Wassat Mom?

I stopped in my tracks as we walked down the quiet lane from the cottage.

What the heck is it?

I was not putting a paw any further until I knew what that thing on the road was. It was big, about four chickens high and three chickens fat with short legs. It turned to look in our direction. It had a flat face on a head like a bowling ball. It was weird. It was also pink...ish. There was a lot of mud on it, too.

Please, Mom, what is it?

"It's okay, Joey, it's a wild pig."

A wild pig? Huh. I wasn't keen on the wild pig, but he was busy munching at a load of cabbage on the road. He made sloppy, wet sounds as he ate and then belched. I wasn't impressed. Mom walked us to the other side of the road, and for once in my life, I kept quiet. Oh my, there's another one of them! It's coming for us! Oh, no, it's not. It's going for the cabbage. Hmmph, okay. I can cope with that.

We walked past the pigs without incident. Being wild, they were used to people walking around them, as demonstrated by a couple coming out of the little shop close to where they were eating and just walking past. The cabbage was far more interesting! They were also right by an old red phone box that had been turned into a library. So, if anyone wanted to look at the books, they had to wait.

I had my Ordnance Survey map of the area in my pocket and knew we could do a short walk around and back through the woods. A couple of miles walk would do us both good. Right and right again, we turned onto a track that ran next to the woods. Although the sun was shining, the woods were so dense; they were dark and gloomy and, to be fair, a little frightening. The next gate we came across that led into the woods was locked, which was unusual. Then I read the sign on the gate: 'No entry. Rare mushrooms. No Foraging'. The Forestry Commission did its best to preserve the rare fungi growing here. Further on, the gate was open, and people were allowed to forage. Not that I was about to: my knowledge of wild mushrooms is limited to the shaggy ink cap, and I won't pick those unless I'm with someone who knows what they are doing!

As we got back to the cottage, the evening was drawing in. With muddy boots removed and left outside to dry off, I towelled Joey down before making our last supper in the cottage. Tomorrow, we were heading home.

Chapter Thirty-One

We were a happy little team with just the two of us. We settled into a nice routine of walks, work, and trips away. Joey was popular wherever we went and loved by everyone, especially children. He enjoyed all the attention and the fuss. The one thing he did miss was male company. I wasn't particularly bothered about dating, and after a twenty-four-year marriage, I enjoyed being me.

The odd date did happen, and Joey always enjoyed the male company; in fact, he was a complete tart! I'm sure he was giving any guy I dated puppy dog eyes, but no one set the spark alight in mine.

The significant change in my life was selling my small business: that was enough to concentrate on for the time being! I allowed myself a twelve-month break from work to do as I pleased and to get rid of the stress I had been under for the last thirty years. It was a valuable time of recovery. I was never bored; there were plenty of things to do and places to travel with Joey. We had a great time.

After selling my business, I enjoyed almost twelve months of freedom, but money was getting tight. With a mortgage that still needed paying, I took a regular 9-5 job as an Activity Coordinator in a dementia care home. This would be a big learning curve for both Joey and me. We had barely been apart for more than four or five hours since we had met.

Thank heavens for good neighbours. Joey was as good as gold when left at home, and Jayne, our neighbour, offered to go around at lunchtime and let him out. It was typical of Joey to enjoy Jayne's visits, as he got extra fuss and treats.

At this time, I was an admin on a Facebook group for travellers with pets. It found and highlighted caravan and camping sites around the UK that fit the bill. We were a friendly bunch of admins who bantered with each other daily and monitored the page. We followed each other's travels and always discussed our doggy pals. Joey and I were just about to go on holiday, so my administrative duty was relinquished for a week.

We were off on holiday again, yeah. I wondered where we were going this time. It was hot, and I could smell the countryside. Did that mean I was going to see some boppies?

Mom pulled onto a site and got out to book in. With the windows wide open, I felt a lovely cool breeze entering my shady seat. It was lovely. I looked into the woods at the side of us, my eyes trying to detect any movement, but I could only see birds.

We were in Hereford. It is a beautiful, unspoiled area

of England that is close to the border of Wales. I recall visiting the town as a teenager with my parents while camped at the Malvern Hills. My Dad and I would make a beeline for the cattle market in the town centre and enjoy browsing along the pens of cattle stock and sheep. My mother feared bulls for some reason, so she steered well clear of those. While Dad and I were there leaning on the railings admiring these fantastic beasts, Mom roamed among the sheep pens.

The site I booked was outside the town in the beautiful green countryside.

"Okay, Joey, let's find a pitch." It was a roasting July day, and we needed a pitch with some shade. The site was very open, and the only trees to give any shade at all were around the outer perimeter. I checked the sun's position and chose a pitch across the back hedge by a tree. We would get some shade from that, at least. I parked up, plugged in the electrics and gave Joey some water. Phew, it was cooler in the Berlingo! We don't usually get summers like this, and it promised to be a scorcher all week. I quickly popped the tent up, hoping to give more shade, before flopping down by the side of the van with a cold bottle of water. Joey, quite sensibly, was half underneath, looking quite relaxed, lucky boy.

That evening's meal was a hearty salad with a nice cold glass of Pinot Grigio. It felt good to be sitting outside on a proper summer's evening. I always feel so relaxed sitting outdoors in the shade, just watching the world go by, and it was made even better with the company of Joey. He sat by my side, nose twitching for any scent of interest and eyes scanning the open campsite before us. It was perfect.

We were up early the following day as it was predicted to be another hot one. I walked Joey through the woods and was aghast to see some caravaners in the more shaded area with an electric fan on in their awning! Some people amaze me. Joey and I were happy to laze away the first day of our holiday, moving around from shady spot to shady spot, enjoying the odd breeze when it whistled through the hedge and the trees. We were both content.

We were on the grassy area of the site, and there was only one other campervan nearby whom we had yet to meet. The whole week we were there, we saw him only once.

Today, we could have a visitor, and I was looking forward to having company. A motorhome pulled into the next pitch as we lazed around in the late afternoon, enjoying the cooler temperatures. It was David from the Facebook group with his dog Jake, a Cocker Spaniel. This area was midway on his journey home, and he had asked if I minded him turning up for the night to break his journey.

Oh, who is this? Woohoo, it's a man; I hope he likes dogs. And look at his kennel, it's enormous compared to ours! I came out of my shady spot and headed towards the man with my best puppy dog eyes and wagging tail, and I couldn't help myself; I barked. The man was straight down to me and giving me a big fuss. Oh, how did he know I liked to be scratched behind my ears? I was in heaven; I liked this man!

Then a bonus! A black bundle of floof came running out of the motorhome to greet me. The man not only knew I liked a fuss, but he had a fluffy buddy, too!

"This is Jake," said David. "He's very friendly."

Jake sniffed my bum, so I sniffed his. We both wagged our tails and started playing.

It's always good to meet fellow campers in the flesh, so to speak, when you've been friends on Facebook for some time, although I did feel a little intimidated with Joey and me in our Berlingo and David and Jake in his large motorhome. The big bonus for Joey and me was that the shadow cast by his motorhome was much better than any shadow we had previously managed to attain, so we were both in heaven sitting there whilst David insisted on cooking a paella.

Whilst cooking and chatting, we heard a man's voice cursing. Neither of us could work out where it was coming from. Weirdly, it seemed to be coming from the sky! The cursing continued, and we could hear a sound like the flapping canvas of a tent. Then, out of the corner of my eye, it all became apparent. A hang glider came into view over the field next to us, and he was struggling with his wing. He landed in an ungainly heap in the freshly ploughed field with more cussing and expletives. As we watched through the gaps in the hedge, we elected that, as he was moving okay and still cursing, we would leave him to deal with it unless he asked for our help.

The poor guy must have been gutted that he had landed where he had. He collected his kit and began walking to the bottom of the field. At that point, I shouted that he couldn't get out that way, but I was ignored. Ten minutes later, he came tromping back up the field to find another way through. This time, we asked if he wanted a hand and were, as expected, ignored. I wondered where he was supposed to be and how he would get home: once he found a way out of the field, that is!

It was dinner time for Jake and me, and we both ate with gusto. However, I was not too happy when Jake ignored his own water bowl and drank out of mine. He slobbered, leaving drool in the bowl and spraying it everywhere. Where were this chap's manners? I would not drink that again until Mom changed it for fresh water!

David and I chatted late into the evening with the dogs curled up at our feet before going to bed. They were gone by the time we got up in the morning, and we hadn't heard them leave. We would miss that extra shade as the days were getting hotter.

There was no point in going out anywhere as it was far too hot. But I wasn't complaining. Life had been so busy that it was nice to laze and read or draw. I doused spare towels in water for Joey to lie on or have over him and kept us both hydrated. Only when the cool of the evening came did we exert ourselves for a decent walk. I was so glad to have the wood right by us as it offered continual shade. It was just a shame that there was nowhere on the edge of it where we could sit during the day. I'd even rigged the windbreak canvas across the rear door of the Berlingo to give us a little extra shade: washing pegs have many uses, I thought as I clipped the canvas in place.

I did toy with the idea of moving elsewhere or going home early, but the last thing I wanted to do was have Joey in a hot car unless necessary. It was a holiday with little to tell other than it was blooming hot!

Chapter Thirty-Two

I thoroughly enjoyed the job in the care home, even though it was incredibly demanding, both mentally and physically. I had to create enriching activities for those living with dementia. It stretched my capabilities, but I loved it. Skye, the PAT dog [Pets As Therapy], was a regular visitor. She was a lovely Golden Retriever who would go and visit all the residents and sit very happily whilst they gave her some fuss. Obedient unless she found cake crumbs on someone's lap or the floor! She was a complete star, and the residents greatly benefited from her visits. I decided to pop in with Joey on a Saturday and cleared it with the Manager. I was convinced he would love it.

This is a big house! Oh, hang on, before we go in, I need a pee! We went in through big doors, and there were loads of people. I was soon surrounded by countless hands giving me lots of fuss: I liked it here. Mom took me around to meet people who lived there. Some were asleep in their chairs, and others' eyes lit up when they saw me coming. I was gently placed on some people's laps for a fuss and received a lot of kisses and gave lots back in return. We even went in a moving box that Mom called a lift and saw even more people. I really enjoyed it, but it was very tiring.

Joey had been a star visiting all the residents at the care home, and we stopped downstairs for a drink of water for him and a cup of tea for me before we left. He had been a dream with everyone and hadn't shown an urge to cock his leg up anywhere once, which was a big relief for me. I knew now that he would be tired, though, so once more out into the garden for a pee, and then we headed home, knowing that both he and the residents had had a great sensory experience.

Chapter Thirty-Three

David and I stayed in touch and eventually became a couple. Our first camping trips together were spent in our independent vans, but it was great that David always volunteered to cook, although I did take along meals that I had prepared at home, too, so we had a choice. Joey was in heaven and was entirely under David's spell. He would do anything for him: within reason!

It's the lovely man again! I'm going into his big kennel this time to see how cosy it is. While he and Mom were talking, I hopped up the steps to his motorhome and straight onto the seat: this was heavenly. Mom and David followed me in, and Mom was very apologetic that I had made myself so comfy without being asked.

"Joey, you are a terror! I'm so sorry, David."

Mom had her hands under my bum to move me, but I was pretending to be asleep and wasn't going to shift. It was far too snug.

"Don't worry, I'm quite happy that Joey is comfy here; he's a lovely boy."

Hearing that, I relaxed, stretched out, and genuinely went to sleep; it was so cosy.

We had a lovely few days in the sunshine: great food, good company, and fantastic weather. We had walked from the site into St Neots and lunched at a very dog-friendly pub by the river. As my Berlingo took all of five minutes to pack and be ready for the road, I said I'd help David pack his away when I'd finished. While I was doing this, Joey was curled up inside on the seat.

"Be careful going in and out, David; Joey is a little Houdini."

"It's Okay; it's fine. The screen door is across, so he can't get out."

We continued to pack away, and I heard David slide the screen door across to get inside.

"Oh, you little bugger!"

Joey had escaped.

I grabbed his lead and watched him race around in circles on the site.

"Joey! Come here, come on!"

I knew there was no point in running after him; he would see it as a game. Round and round, he ran, then headed for the open door of a caravan. He darted inside and then back out again. He was having the time of his life and totally ignored me!

He stopped to sniff and pee, then looked up at me, gave a woof, and headed off again. My heart was racing. I knew I'd get hold of him, but when? Thankfully, we were well off the road, but we had a fast-flowing river nearby and a path into the woods that led into the park and town. I was beginning to panic.

"David, if you go into the edge of the woods, I'll stay behind him. Hopefully, he will see you and stop."

David headed off, and Joey followed suit.

"Got him!"

I ran to the woods to see a relieved David and a panting Joey. I slipped on his lead and gave him a few stern words as we walked back onto the campsite.

"I know you said he could be a Houdini, but that gap was so tiny that he got through."

"Now you know, but I need a cup of tea to calm down."

Joey? Happy as anything. Eyes shining and still excited, he had a drink of water and lay down for a rest.

This wasn't the only occasion that he did his escapology act either! A few months later, we were camping at Kingsbury Water Park. As I was working on Friday, David was going Friday lunchtime to set up, and I would drive straight there from work. I'd altered my hours that week and left 2 hours early so we could enjoy the weekend. I arrived on site to a frazzled David.

"What's wrong?" I asked as I saw him bashing the stakes of the windbreak. "And where is Joey?"

With a bash of the mallet, David turned and said, "The little sod got out. I was coming out the door to do the windbreak while he was asleep on his bed. What I didn't realise was that he wasn't asleep at all. When I opened the door, he shot out and ran like a mad thing possessed. He went through that row of caravans and headed to the grass area, where he ran around in circles, barking before catching the scent of something and heading to the hedge. I grabbed his lead and some treats and began calling him. He looked at me, then carried on running around."

At this point, I was trying hard not to giggle.

"I decided to head him off at the top of the field before the gate to the lane, where I eventually managed to get the lead on to him."

Now, I did giggle. "I did warn you, and you know what he's like!" David looked very frustrated. "Ah well, you caught him, and he won't need a long walk tonight!"

David was doubly cautious the rest of the weekend when going out the van door!

Oh, that was a great run around. Don't really know why Dad was so worried. I'd have come back when I'd had my fun! And why was Mom so stressed about it all? I'd have come back when I wanted to: after I'd chased boppies and said hello to people. Humans do worry about things!

Chapter Thirty-Four

Camping-well, if you can call it that in the luxury of a motorhome-was a large part of our lives. With David already retired, for the third time, we got away as often as we could.

We would love to let Joey off in a secure area, but being so small, many of these areas needed to be more secure for Joey. If a cat could get through a mesh fence, so could he.

We had gone to a large commercial site in Yorkshire with a two-acre field just for the dogs: now that is doggy heaven. Pitched up for a week with some friends, we decided to brave the dog field. Joey was good with most dogs now, so we went into the field. There was a gap under the gate, big enough for Joey to get under, but I figured he would be more interested in the rest of the field to worry about that. It was huge and sloping up a small hill, with good visibility across the field. We didn't make a fuss about letting him off; we just released the clip on the lead and continued to walk on.

Ooh, there are lots of sniffs here and tons of peemails. This is great. As I went, I ambled on, sniffing and answering peemails, then realised that Mom was not behind me. I stopped. Where was she? When I turned to look, I realised that she was standing still and that I had no lead attached to me. Whoopee, I was free, time for a run. I ran, and I ran, up to the top corner of the field and then along the top. Oh my, there were so many sniffs for me to stop at; I was so excited I stopped to bark and then ran some more. I stopped, looked back at Mom and Dad, and wagged my tail; this was so much fun! I could hear them calling me, but I pretended I couldn't hear them. This was too good an opportunity to miss. I started going down the other side of the field; I could smell boppies. Where were those boppies? I put my nose through the hedge and fence in various places: they must be in the woods on the other side. Now, where can I get through to get to them? Mom, shut up! I can hear you, but this is more important!

"He's not taking any ruddy notice, David. I'm sure he's trying to get through that hedge into the woods."

"Blooming hope not; it'd take us ten minutes to get to where he is now. There's no chance if he gets through."

"All I can see is the white tip of his tail wagging like mad."

As we wondered how to deal with this, a lady with two border collies entered the field.

"Good morning, beautiful day, isn't it?" she said as she started to unclip her dogs from their leads.

"It's lovely; we just wish our dog would return from the top of the field."

The lady was scanning the field. "What type of dog? I can't see anything at all."

"Top left, looks like a smaller version of your two."

With that, Joey was looking our way, so I called him again.

There was a peak of interest as he saw the border collies. Within seconds, he decided that they were interesting and came bounding down the field.

"Would you mind," I asked, "if he comes near you, could you grab him for me, please?"

He finally reached us and went straight up to the lady and her dogs, and I managed to get the lead on him.

"Thank you, you appeared at the right time!"

Joey was standing there, panting and wagging his tail. He had had fun and certainly wanted more of it! Instead, it was a walk back to the motorhome and a large drink of water; then, he crashed out in the shade. He was twitching paws in his sleep, dreaming of his exploits, no doubt.

If we had the car with us while we were away, we visited small towns or nice locations of historical interest. Joey always displayed his best behaviour when visiting ruins and castles. He happily ambled alongside us, sniffing here and there. If we stopped for tea or in a pub, he shamelessly harvested head scratches or lay down quite happily. He was a perfect pub dog. It was never long before he got people's attention as they walked past him. With those appealing puppy dog eyes and wagging tail, they were hooked. Joey, of course, suffered all the fuss he could get.

The conversations always went similar to the following.

"Oh, she is such a beautiful puppy; how old is she?"

"He's twelve [enter any age up to eighteen here as it was a regular statement]."

"He really is cute. Twelve months?" [Note the person happily fussing, picking up on the gender.]

"No, twelve years."

"Oh my, is he a miniature Border Collie?"

"No, he's half Cocker Spaniel and half Sheltie." We always clarified that he wasn't a designer breed, just an accidental cross.

"What a beautiful boy he is. You're lucky to have one that's so cute."

"He can be a little devil, don't be fooled by the cuteness level!"

Some days, we could have this conversation many, many times. The most I recall in one day was eighteen times. We used to lay odds on it happening before we went anywhere new.

Going into small towns was great and amusing as long as it wasn't too busy: Joey was easily missed on the pavement amongst legs and pushchairs. We always tried to go when it was quieter or skirt the busy points. For whatever reason, Joey always got excited in small towns and villages. He would have a pee, then raise his head and give a series of little barks whilst wagging his tail. He skipped around a bit, barked again, and settled into a jaunty walk. He always looked so happy, and he certainly made people smile. You could see his happiness; it was nice to know that he brought so much joy to people's lives other than our own.

Chapter Thirty-Five

We were packing to go away [again!], and Joey, as usual, had to have his nose into everything. David had just returned from shopping, and we were unpacking and putting things away when I heard a rustling sound. I turned around and fell about laughing. Joey had put his head into one of the empty shopping bags. He had done so by entering the bag through the handle. Every time he tried to back out of the bag, the bag went with him. He looked utterly perplexed at this thing, and he could not escape! Once untangled, he went to lie on the back of the chair and people watch: obviously, it wasn't as much fun bag sniffing as he thought.

With the van packed, we were off to Highlands End Campsite in Dorset to meet up with friends from Motorhome Fun. It wasn't an organised rally; everyone was scattered across the site, and we all just met when wandering around and chatting. As we were sitting outside, one new member appeared and introduced herself as Claire. Chatty and friendly, she was trying to meet up with fellow members. I know how hard it is to leap into the unknown, and we invited her back later for a drink if the weather held.

There was a knock on the door just after tea, and there was Claire, complete with a glass, a chair, and a bottle of wine, but there was someone else. She had persuaded the girl next door, Rachel, to come over, too. She also had a glass, chair, wine, and a large dog: a mastiff weighing 84kg. I mention this because Joey is a monster of nine kilos, and sometimes, he was still a bit nervous around big dogs. What he would make of a massive mastiff remained to be seen.

Popping on fleeces, we sat around outside, making introductions with Rachel and Elsa. Elsa promptly lay down, leant up the windbreak, and knocked it over: she did not know her size. Joey and Elsa saying hello would be an interesting introduction. When I first adopted Joey, he was fearful of anything much bigger than he was. I was concerned about how this could go. But then it happened. Joey and Elsa set eyes on each other, and it was magical: they fell in love.

Elsa lay down, and Joey tentatively approached her. They were nose to nose. Elsa was thumping her tail on the ground hard enough to cause an earthquake, and Joey's tail was wagging so fast it was a blur. Then Elsa stood up; I held my breath. I was thinking of the time he met Jet, the Newfoundland. Joey looked up and then up again, straining his neck to reach Elsa's nose.

Then he went into a downward dog yoga pose, closely

followed by Elsa doing the same. A large paw came out and bopped Joey on the head; he thought it was great! But knowing the power of a larger dog, we elected to draw them apart. Elsa was only 18 months old; I don't think she knew her strength.

It was late when we went inside to go to bed. Our coats and blankets that we had used over our knees were thrown into a heap on the one bench seat. Joey went straight onto his bed, curled up and fell asleep.

I got up the following day and couldn't see Joey. I looked at his bed, assuming he had stayed there all night, but he wasn't there. This was confusing and worrying. Where was he? I called his name, and the jumble of coats began to move. With another call, his little nose poked out from amongst the coats, and then he started panting. He had snuggled in there very nicely but was now hot and struggling to get out. What an idiot.

Sadly, none of us took a photo of the love birds, and Rachel and Elsa had left early in the morning. Poor Joey sniffed daily at the grass where she had lain after that: love's young dream.

The following day, once the wind had died down, I was happily basking in the sun with my eyes shut, David was reading, and Joey was laid out enjoying the sun on his belly when we heard a voice say something about a cat. A cat? Oh lord, if Joey catches sight of a cat, he'll pull me off the chair. I opened my eyes to see a family looking behind us as they spoke about the cat.

"Where's the cat?"

"Your cat," they exclaimed.

"We don't have a cat."

The lady pointed, "The one lying beside you."

I looked down at Joey, "No, that's a dog."

To which Joey pops his head up.

"Oh, I'm sorry! The way he was lying there looking so fluffy, we thought he was a cat."

Walking the cat, sorry, Joey, later, I saw a little boy on his tiny bike. He had been on it regularly, but the minute he lifted his feet off the ground, he wobbled and fell off. Dad asked if he wanted stabilisers.

"No, Dad, I can do it," would be the repeated reply.

Dad was helping him to get going again, calling, "Pedal, pedal, I've got you." Within minutes, the little one was pedalling furiously on his own and getting a round of applause from the family and us, too. Even Joey joined in with a happy bark and a tail wag.

Chapter Thirty-Six

One of David's keen interests is British Phantom Aircraft, a great piece of aviation history, so I'm told. His grandfather had a hand in the McDonald Douglas ejector seat, and he was now a helpful enthusiast who would drive up and down the country to help restore Black Mike.

Quoted courtesy of bpag.co.uk: "It's safe to say that due to its record-setting achievements and its unique colour scheme, XV582 'Black Mike' could be one of the most famous aircraft that the Royal Air Force has ever flown. There is also much support for the claim that it is the second most famous Phantom in the world. All of this makes it surprising to learn that the aircraft was virtually abandoned by the RAF when they vacated the base at Leuchars, Scotland, in 2015 and left it behind. It was only due to a heroic effort by the British Phantom Aviation Group that XV582 escaped the scrapman's axe."

The first time Joey and I got involved with the restoration guys was at Cockpit Fest at Newark Air Museum.

Whilst David was happy on the stand, Joey and I would go on walks, or we could relax, and I could catch up on some writing. It made for a lovely weekend for all of us.

It was my first time meeting the guys, and at last, I could put faces to names I'd only heard about in conversation. Well, the guys met Joey, and he was spoiled rotten. Joey knew he had them all eating out of his paw-even those who said they didn't like dogs!

Joey took centre stage When we sat outside for our evening meal. He worked the room by going to one person, wagging and giving puppy dog eyes in the hope of getting a treat before repeating at the next gullible person. Bits of sausage were tendered, providing he sat and gave a paw. Once he had done an entire circuit, he curled up next to one of the guys and slept off his full belly. He was such a hit with the guys that the following year, no one was bothered about David or me turning up; they all wanted to see Joey.

One of the guys in particular, Mike, formed a powerful bond with Joey. Mike was very much a man's-man, but when he saw Joey, he was putty in his paws. Evening meals were round at our van as we had the amenities for cooking, and Joey would, sooner or later, end up on Mike's lap or in his dog bed at his feet, happily snuggled under a blanket when the evening got chillier. Once more, Joey was making people happy by just being Joey, and he quickly became the BPAG Cockpit Fest Mascot.

Chapter Thirty-Seven

After two years of working in a dementia care home, I changed my career. I had taken a role at the local college, so my holidays were the same as the students. It was perfect after the gruelling days of being self-employed and long weeks working in care. It allowed us to use the motorhome much more and for longer periods.

Lincolnshire was an area we had never been to. We managed to book a week in Sutton on Sea at a small site run by the owner of Motorhome Fun called Jim. A friendly group of motorhome owners from around the UK and Europe who met up throughout the year at motorhome shows and rallies. It was a glorious week in July, and as we had towed the car, we could get out and about.

We sat outside one evening enjoying the sunshine, David dozing in the chair, I was reading a book, and Joey was enjoying the breeze ruffling his fur when, out of the corner of my eye, I saw something move under the edge of the motorhome. It was one of Jim's chickens who had escaped from the coop. She was clucking away as she approached Joey's food bowls.

I glanced across at Joey, who, thankfully, was totally oblivious. I dared not move, as I didn't want to cause mayhem, but I managed to slide my foot over Joey's lead so that he couldn't go far if he did wake up. The chicken blinked and clucked, then hopped onto Joey's water bowl and helped herself to a drink! Joey raised his head, looked, thought better of it, and went back to sleep!

Some days were too hot to go anywhere with Joey, but we were content lazing in the shade and chatting to fellow campers. While driving around, we both appreciated how beautiful Lincolnshire was and that house prices were much cheaper than in the Midlands or down south. We had never really talked about moving, but we were seriously thinking about it now. We knew several people who had relocated to the area, and we began working out what we could afford.

The great revelation was that I could give up work if we did move and follow my dream of being a full-time writer and artist. We slept on it for a few months but kept our eyes open on the property market until I came home from work one day to the announcement from David that he had booked three viewings in a couple of days, so we would be back off to Sutton on Sea for the weekend! With a three-and-a-half hour trip each way, it was going to be tiring, but at least in the motorhome, it reduced accommodation costs. The criteria were flexible; the dream was to have space for the motorhome and cars on the front so we didn't have to have the motorhome in storage. We wanted to be located rurally or semi-rurally but near enough to towns for shopping.

Lincolnshire is the second largest county in England, with Yorkshire being the largest. A large proportion of the area is flat land surrounding the Wolds, which have idyllic rolling hills. There are fields as far as the eye can see, and roads, somewhat strangely for those of us from further south, don't tend to have hedges along the fields. There is something much more dangerous to the motorist: a ditch! Commonly known as soak dikes, they take any water that soaks through from the rivers, hence the term. Pulling onto a verge in Lincolnshire has to be done with care. With most areas being so flat, there is plenty of warning to choose a suitable spot for passing.

Driving over, we had a phone call. The first property we were due to look at in Spilsby had been sold that morning. That was disappointing as we had walked past this property on a previous visit. We loved the look of it, and it was right on the edge of the town, so an easy walk to the shops. It looked like a barn conversion and had been restored sensitively. Car parking would have been tight, but as we had seen it in the flesh from the outside, we figured out a way to get the vehicles behind the gates: by getting rid of the beautiful large flowerbed to the side! Never mind, what was meant to be was meant to be: onto the next one.

House number two was on the outskirts of Mablethorpe and a bungalow. Mablethorpe is a coastal town close to Skegness. It has a busy and thriving centre and a long golden sandy beach. There are holiday parks one after the other, and during the high season, it is a favourite spot with tourists. The house we were going to look at was as far away from this element of Mablethorpe as you could get. On the edge of Mablethorpe on a lovely tree-lined road. It would not be my favourite area if I were to list them, but it was away from the main seafront, and the drive was across a little stream. It was very rural and in a perfect location. From the outside, it looked great.

We met the estate agent and went inside. What a disappointment. I stood in the kitchen doorway and felt the floor giving way beneath my feet. I bounced up and down, and the floor moved an inch or two. This prompted David to move around, and his doorway sprang even more. The estate agent said nothing. We progressed to the outside and looked up to see bare cables leading across to the garage and around from the front door, then back into the front bedroom. This was near the top of our budget, and we both mentally racked up thousands of pounds in repairs before we could declare the place habitable.

It was then I realised Joey needed a pee, but there was nowhere safe to walk dogs. Once off the drive, you were onto the road, and it was a busy cut-through for locals to avoid going through the town centre. This one was a definite no for both of us.

House number three was a modern bungalow much nearer to Mablethorpe's main attractions. As we had been back to the site, we left Joey in the motorhome for this next visit. This was a very modern estate, purpose-built for the elderly, and the bungalow we were looking at was on a considerable corner plot with double gates so the motorhome could go into the back garden. The outside space was huge.

The couple, who were moving to a flat on the seafront, were keen gardeners and had their caravan between lovely flowerbeds. I think we both had visions of driving over the beautifully manicured beds! Plus, neither of us has any inclination to maintain a garden so beautiful. Sadly, the interior was far too small for us, which was a shame because it was immaculate. The kitchen did not have enough room for one person to cook, let alone two and a nosey dog. Whoever bought that one would have a lovely home to walk into and enjoy, but it wasn't for us.

Feeling a bit despondent, we stopped off at Waldo's chippy in Sutton on Sea before heading back to the motorhome around the corner and discussing our thoughts on the day. Although none of the properties had been for us, it had enforced our thoughts that Lincolnshire was a great place to call home.

Back at our current home and back to work, it was hard not to say anything to the rest of the college team. We were a tightly knit bunch, but I didn't want to face a barrage of questions about what we planned to do. It was so difficult to keep my mouth shut!

The following week, I came home from work, and David said he had found a huge bungalow further north in a little village. He had booked to view it and was going to drive up and see what it was like, then drive back in one day. I encouraged him to take an overnight bag just in case he needed to stop over anywhere if he found something else whilst he was in the area. Lincolnshire seemed so far away from Worcestershire to be doing the drive there and back in one day.

"It's massive," he said when he came in the door on his return, "the lounge is huge, and there's plenty of room for the vehicles. It is a lovely corner plot and a decent back garden, too. It needs work, but looks good."

Guess where we trooped off to the following weekend? Yup, back up to Lincolnshire for a second viewing. Joey was quite happy with this toing and froing. He was quite content in the back seat. We stopped halfway for a break, and then he would go back to sleep again. It was also nice to see other parts of Lincolnshire: it really was beautiful. The northeast of Lincolnshire was far less touristy than lower down the coast. The village David had located was just a fifteen-minute drive from Grimsby and Cleethorpes, and it had a good feel about it. We were feeling quite positive.

The estate agent was already there when we arrived and we were early.

"I just need to walk Joey, and then we will be in."

I got a look. "Your appointment is for only fifteen minutes; I can't hang around."

"My dog has been in the car for over three hours; he needs to stretch his legs!"

This was not a good start!

I put Joey back into the car after he had done his thing and went into the bungalow. It was, as David had said, massive. The L-shaped lounge was bigger than the downstairs of my current house, but the fire was placed in the tiny bit of the L. There were two huge patio windows overlooking the rear garden, but someone had painted the glass on one of the enormous windows to block the afternoon sun. Looking around we noticed a few water leak stains on the ceilings.

"David?"

"What?"

"Look at this."

I pointed to a considerable crack that ran down one of the walls where they had extended the lounge. We looked at each other but said nothing to the agent.

Opening the back door, I was engulfed in the noise from the A16 that ran behind the house. The property had been empty for a while, so the garden was a tad on the wild side.

"Nice garden."

"Oh, you like gardening?"

"No, not at all, but it has some nice features." That shut the snotty woman up!

"I'll leave you to look at the outside as there are no gates or anything. Nice to meet you." She locked the bungalow, and she was gone.

Personally, I hoped we never met again. Some people can just rub you up the wrong way from the get-go. I got Joey out of the car as soon as she had gone.

Joey enjoyed sniffing around the garden and left his mark in a few places. Again, the house needed a lot of work to make it habitable, and that considerable crack worried me.

"David, the garage door is open."

We went inside, and to our horror, the other side of the crack we had seen in the lounge was there: subsidence.

"What do you think of the place?"

"Honestly? I hate it. The lounge is a huge, badly configured space that needed redesigning to make it workable. The roof needs attention; the whole place needs decorating, new double glazing, and that crack—who knows how much that was going to be to rectify? Then there's the noise from the main road. I've lived on a dual carriageway before and never again."

David was slightly deflated, even though he knew I was talking sense. It was far too big a project for us. As we left, we decided to walk Joey around and see if there was anything else in the area.

"There's another one over the road and around the corner, and it's in a much better condition and looks nice."

We both wandered towards it and stood looking at it.

"I'll give the agent a call."

Unfortunately, the agent couldn't come out to do a viewing right then, so we all piled back into the car, drove to a service station, grabbed something light to eat, and headed back to the Midlands.

Joey may be fine sleeping in the back of the car, but this house-viewing lark that wasn't on your doorstep was proving to be tiring work. We were knackered!

Guess where we went the following weekend? Yes, back onto Jim's site at Sutton on Sea, with that house to view and another one we had spotted online. We weren't particularly looking forward to the first viewing as it was the same estate agent as the previous one with the snotty woman, but fingers crossed, she may have gotten out of bed on the right side this time.

Thankfully, a different agent turned up. He was a lovely man who helped David measure the drive to see if the motorhome fitted and also took a shine to Joey. He was happy for us to bring Joey into the house. As he said, he was going to live there, too, so it was good to see his reaction.

Again, this was a bungalow of a far better standard than the previous one around the corner. The avocado bath suite needed changing, but it was all well-kept and functional. You also couldn't hear much of the road noise here either, which was a bonus. This one was undoubtedly liveable whilst we made minor changes and upgraded the electrics. It was nice and bright, with big windows and a decent-sized kitchen. Being a corner plot, the small rear garden was a bonus as neither of us is a keen gardener, and the front had plenty of room for us to expand the drive to allow better space for parking. This one ticked a lot of boxes.

We had an hour or two before the next viewing, so we meandered around the area to see if there were any other properties we liked the look of. We visited nearby villages, but we soon realised that those villages didn't have the same feel as this one. If we hadn't found the house for us yet, we had found a location we loved.

We moved on to our last viewing for the day, a dormer bungalow. I was a bit uncertain about this one, primarily because of the deep blue wall in the lounge. Much to my surprise, it was much nicer than I had anticipated. The house inside was immaculate, and the rooms were a good size. The back garden wasn't too big, and the front was huge.

The bonus was that it was all gravelled, and we could easily fit the motorhome and the cars. Although this was more expensive than the other one, it ticked the boxes with stronger ticks! The vast shower sold it to us both. It's funny what draws you to a property. Never in a million years would I have had a massive shower on my list of must-haves.

We thanked the vendor and the agent and went back to the van for a chat and to weigh up the pros and cons of each property. We both decided that the dormer bungalow was a good fit, but we only made an offer once we were home.

The drive back home didn't seem so long this time, as we had a lot of plans to make for the future. But getting up for work on Monday morning was hard!

Offer made.

Offer accepted.

My house was put on the market.

And still, I kept my mouth shut at work! It was not easy knowing I would leave this great bunch of people.

Exchange day was whilst I was still at work, so David went up alone to get the keys and move his stuff in on his birthday. It was a birthday present with a difference for him! It felt strange going on as usual as David set up our future home.

Once I resigned from my job, life was a lot easier. The end of term was just a few days away, and all the students had made me lovely cards. It was both a sad and happy time, but I was off to new adventures, and I was looking forward to them.

Chapter Thirty-Eight

Tidying and clearing my house was a nightmare. I had lived there for sixteen years and used every available space. It was one of the hottest summers we had ever had, and I was ruthlessly going through things as I packed. We didn't need any of my furniture apart from a couple of pieces I wanted to keep for sentimental reasons as they had belonged to my parents. As my purchasers were first-time buyers, they were only too grateful to have most of the furniture, so it was just packing the personal clutter I hadn't binned or given away. I found it very liberating to give things away to people.

What was Mom doing? Boxes of all shapes and sizes surround us. To get to my bed, I had to weave between three towers of them; it made me a nice little hidey-hole, though. Then she threw the spare quilt on the floor. Mom turned her back for a few minutes to reach something else, and I was on it! It was soft and cosy, and I didn't want to get off! Dad then disappeared with boxes to put in the car; I had no idea where he was going! In fact, I had no idea what was going on, but Mom and Dad seemed happy, so I was, too.

It was moving day. David had spent the last few weeks commuting between both houses; thankfully, he enjoyed driving. It was time for the penultimate journey to our new life, leaving Redditch behind.

We loaded as many boxes as possible into the motorhome; the removal company will take the rest before the exchange date on my property. As I had now finished work, we were ready for the off.

We drove to the motorhome storage depot on a hot summer's day. The tow car was hitched up, and I was going to drive the other car in convoy. It was going to be an interesting journey. We had filled the second car with stuff, too, allowing Joey a load of space on the back seat and with the air-con pointed in his direction. We would only be back now to deal with my removals and hand the keys over.

It was a long and careful drive with strategic water stops. With it being so hot, the air conditioning was a relief for all of us. It was a relief when the village we were calling home appeared.

We were too tired after the long journey to unpack anything. All we had to do now was unhitch the tow car and for David to get the motorhome onto the drive. Was it going to fit? With a couple of shunts, it was in place. Both cars were added to the drive, and Joey got out to see his new home.

Hmmm...this is different, I thought as I walked around the new garden. I could smell different cats from what I was used to, and a dog was barking nearby. I must mark my territory, but I'd really like some food. I'm hungry! I trotted indoors, looking for Mom.

It's been a tiring day, even though I've been curled up in the car snoozing. Something special was happening, but I had no idea what. I needed my dinner before having another nap.

I walked into the lounge. Hmmm, this house smells familiar, but not my familiar. Everything is different, but what can I smell that is recognisable? I sniffed around and jumped up onto the sofa. I know it smells of my buddy Jake, Dad's dog, but he wasn't here. He must have slept on this sofa before it was moved here. I wondered if Jake would be joining us.

Where's my bed, Mom? I looked down at my bed from the sofa and decided to stay where I was for my snooze. With a nice cosy cushion to lean upon and Mom and Dad pottering around, I was content. I was soon in a deep sleep, dreaming of so many strange things from cats to...hang on...what was making my nose twitch? I awoke with a start and blinked the sleep from my eyes. Was that fish I could smell? I needed to investigate.

It had been a tiring trip, so dinner was from the local chip shop: we caught it just in time as it shuts at 8 pm! One of the things we had to get used to living in a village. But my oh my, never has fish and chips tasted so good. The hugest piece of fresh haddock hung over the edge of the plate; it was delicious. Joey had woken from his sleep and was begging for a taste. Well, there was plenty left over to share, so he had a little bit, and I saved the rest until the next day.

"Come on, Joey, up to bed." Joey hadn't explored upstairs yet, and when we lived in Redditch, he slept in the bedroom with us.

Joey came to the bottom of the stairs, thought about it, and then walked back into the lounge.

"That's no good, David. I don't think he likes the bend in the stairs. I'll carry him up."

I called him to me and then picked him up. Thankfully, he was easy to carry. Once we got upstairs, he explored the rooms before finding his bed and curling up to sleep. He was exhausted after such a long day doing nothing.

When morning came, I went down to make tea, closely followed by Joey. So, he would come down but not go up. I opened the back door to let him out while I put the kettle on to boil. After doing what every dog needs to do, he trotted back into the kitchen. Let's see if he would follow me back upstairs. No, he was not interested. He sat at the bottom, looking up for a few minutes before entering the lounge. Only time would tell as to whether he braved the stairs.

The morning walk was a doggie cornucopia of sniffs! Being sixteen now and starting to go deaf, walks weren't very long. To be fair, he probably used more energy in the garden. But the dog walks did bring new doggy friends. A short walk could take anything from fifteen minutes to an hour, depending on who we stopped to chat with. People in the village were so friendly!

Being so close to the seaside was great, but going to Cleethorpes during the summer holiday season wasn't the best idea. We wanted to take Joey to the beach so he could have a good sniff around. We just needed to find the right place to go.

That information came from local dog sitters. They were a lovely couple with a gorgeous cocker spaniel, so I asked them if there was anywhere we could take Joey.

"Oh yes, go down to the Fitties."

"The Fitties? That sounds like a weird place.

Jo laughed. "It's lovely and very quaint. There are two car parks that you can use, and it's the dog-friendly end of the beach all year round."

"Thanks, Jo; I'll Google it when we get back."

I relayed the conversation back to David, who looked it up. Being so new to the area, we had yet to learn what was where.

"Shall we go then?" he said.

"What, now?"

"Yes, why not; it's a beautiful day and not too hot, so let's go and find it."

We all got into the car, set the sat-nav, and off we went. We drove down country lanes through little villages until we came to a large holiday park.

"This can't be right?"

"Let's see, it's down here somewhere according to the directions."

We drove slowly over the speed bumps and past the

entrance to Thorpe Holiday Park. Hordes of people walked down the pavement laden with beach balls, games, and towels. Small children in buggies were brandishing buckets and spades, and they were all going in the opposite direction to us. They were heading for the central area of Cleethorpes.

Cleethorpes has managed to retain quite an old-fashioned seaside town air. The buildings lining High Cliff Road were three or four-story Victorian dwellings with beautiful wrought iron balconies on the first floor. On the ground floor were shops, takeaways, and restaurants. The closer to the Central Promenade, the more decorated the businesses were with lights and brightly coloured facades.

The Promenade had a short pier that opened in 1873 and a pavilion at the end. Sadly, a fire destroyed this in 1903, but a new one was built in 1905. In the 1980s, it became a nightclub, and more recently, it was taken over by a large fish and chip shop chain. Not that Cleethorpes needed more chip shops, as there seems to be one on every corner!

The distance of the prom from the holiday park is quite some way, but that's not a problem. You can get the Cleethorpes Coast Light Railway. Sadly, shortened now, it can take you part of the journey on its fifteen-inch gauge steam locomotives into Cleethorpes from the

smallest pub on the planet, The Signal Box Inn, to the Leisure Centre. From here, you can hop onto the Lollipop Train, a white road train with carriages that will take you down to the prom and beyond. And yes, as the name implies, every child gets a lollipop!

Turning in the opposite direction to Cleethorpes, we headed towards the holiday park. Over another couple of speed bumps, a group of young adults were walking along, of an age that they were probably on their first holiday away together and not with their parents.

"David, look, they're wearing 'Kiss Me Quick' hats!" I giggled, "I haven't seen those since the seventies!" We continued past the holiday park and around the bend.

I don't know whether you have read the Narnia books by C.S. Lewis, where the children enter another world through a wardrobe. I felt we had just done this by going round the last bend. We had driven into Humberston Fitties, commonly known as The Fitties, and returned to the 1920s. There are just over three hundred chalet-style buildings on this plotland, that was originally a salt marsh. Fitties is a Lincolnshire term signifying a salt marsh, hence its name. It was divided into plots, and people initially camped and then built on the plots they leased. This developed into a quirky village of individual chalets constructed mostly of wood. Each chalet has individual characteristics and colours. Some are brown timber with a modern double-glazing update. Others still seem to be the original wood-built cabin and can be a little ramshackle. Nearly all bear trinkets given up by the sea of driftwood and shells. They are a delight to behold as you drive or walk past them.

"Oh, look at that one!" I pointed towards an old chalet that looked original and was kept alive by its owner in its unique state. We wanted to explore inside and imagined it still had 1920s furniture. Like others, the trinkets from the seashore were attached to door frames and windowsills. A bench at the front was made from an old tree trunk. To the side was a wooden porch that was like a seaside grotto. More flotsam and jetsam adorned the walls along with old signs, ropes, life rings and buoys, whelk and scallop shells strung together, tinkling in the breeze. It was a joy of family history.

Joey, by now, was awake. His nose was up to the window, sniffing at the sea air. A soft whine came from his throat. Very gently the tail started to wag as he got more excited, then came a bark. Joey was going to love it down here; thankfully, I had brought the long lead for him so he could run around!

Sniff, sniff, I smell something great! It's salty, fresh, exciting, and whiffs of other dogs. I want to get out of the car now!

We stopped, and Mom got the big red lead and clipped it to my harness. I jumped down from the seat. I knew which way I wanted to go, and I was going. Now! I followed the path that the smell was coming from, with Mom trying to keep up. Dad was on his way, too. I dragged Mom onto the sand, got distracted by a tuft of grass for a minute, and charged off again. I was so happy.

My nose was down, and my tail was up; this was fantastic, and I began to run with the breeze blowing through my fur. I came to a sudden halt when I reached the end of my lead. I turned to Mom and began barking, come on, I want to explore! A few other dogs were around, and they had run out into the sea, but I wasn't bothered. I tried to sniff everything on the sand; it smelled so good!

Mom had caught up with me again, and I started to run; this time, I ran in circles around Mom, barking all the time; it was such fun. Especially when Dad got in the way, and I nearly sent him flying as the long lead caught behind his legs! Round and round in huge circles, I went. Mom was laughing, and Dad was filming it; Mom said something about getting giddy. After about five minutes of this, I stopped. My nose had sniffed something disgusting: a bit of dead crab. Crunch. It tasted awful, but it was mine as I'd found it! Dad tried to take it from me, but he couldn't get it, so I crunched some more!

"Oh, Joey, don't eat stuff like that," I groaned, "they're not good for you!" As much as we tried to get rid of the stinky crab, he wasn't going to let it go.

"I wish I'd brought some treats; we could have swapped! Let's hope he doesn't pick up anything else."

But he did. Tiny clams were everywhere; some were just shells, and others had clams inside. They went by way of the crab and were crunched. Then, with a bark, we were off running in circles again. How this old lad had the energy, I didn't know, but I was sure he would sleep well later!

With his mad zoomies done, Joey was happy to walk along the beach more leisurely before we returned to the car and home. Letting him out of the car into the back garden, Joey went straight into more zoomies! This boy was never going to slow down. Up to the top of the garden, back to the gate. A quick turn, then a leap from the paved area to the grass and around again. He made us so happy with his bunny hop style run, ears flapping as he bounced up and down.

This area became a firm favourite for all of us, and we would try to get down there every week so that Joey could let off some steam and explore. Plus, it was good for us, too.

Chapter Thirty-Nine

If we were away for more than a few days, we often took the tow car (commonly called a toad). The car was a great asset because our large motorhome was not ideal for popping out and seeing the sights.

We were in Bridlington as part of a two-week road trip. Rather than rushing from one place to the next, we stopped for a few nights to see the area. The next day, we were visiting Scarborough. We set off, with Joey settling straight into sleep mode in the back seat.

I had a Facebook friend up here called Gill, who had the ice cream van on the Esplanade. I wondered if she was about today, so I ensured we went along that way in case I could see her. But no joy. It's my fault; I should have messaged her when we set out.

We dropped into the town and hunted for places to park along the coastal road. Nothing; it was packed. I drove past the harbour and followed it left around the bend.

"I'll whip around, and we can go back again and see if we can find somewhere on the other side of the road."

U-turn complete, we crawled slowly back along the road.

"There's one," said David, pointing to the other side of the road where a car was pulling out."

With another quick U-turn and a nifty bit of parallel parking, we were in: thank heavens for small cars.

Joey was wide awake and excited to get out of the car. He could smell the sea.

"As we are near the toilets, I'll pop in before we go anywhere," said David.

"Okay, I'll wait along here for you."

David crossed the road as Joey and I continued to window shop. Well, I window-shopped, and Joey read peemails.

Delicious smells were coming from a busy cafe we were approaching. Joey's nose was going nineteen to the dozen. Food had become important to him as he had gotten older, and he was becoming a terrible scrounge. But then my eye was caught by a lady coming out of the cafe.

It can't be, can it? I thought. What if I call her name and it isn't her? I'd look like an absolute idiot. Another part of me was thinking that if I didn't call her name and it was her, it would be a shame to miss out on meeting up.

"Gill?" I called tentatively. She hadn't heard me.

"Gill?" This time, it was louder, and those sitting at the outside tables turned to see who was calling whom.

This time, the lady turned around with a puzzled expression. "Yes?"

"Gill, it's Alison off Facebook?"

I could see the penny drop as Gill looked down at Joey.

"Joey!"

The tail wagged, and Gill went straight in for cuddles. Then Gill and I hugged.

"My God, fancy meeting you like this!"

"I know; it was completely random, and I was afraid of looking like an idiot if it wasn't you."

We had a lovely chat while we waited for David to come back over the road to be introduced. Eventually, Gill returned to the cafe for her lunch (I hope it hadn't gone too cold by now), but not until Joey had been smothered in cuddles. It was certainly worth the potential of looking like an idiot to meet up!

We continued to have a lovely walk around before perching ourselves on a bench with a coffee. Joey was undoubtedly enjoying this trip as he had a spring in his step. Gill's cuddles had obviously made him happy.

Chapter Forty

We were heading up to Hawick on the Scottish Borders (pronounced 'hoik' by the locals), stopping off in Northumberland near Holy Island and Bamburgh Castle. As dogs weren't allowed in the castle, Joey stayed in the motorhome with the air conditioning on, catching up on sleep while we went sightseeing. The view of the castle as you approach it is impressive. It sits perched on high ground, dominating the skyline. It is stunning and well worth a visit for its historical value and the costumes inside, which were used in filming many films and television series.

After lunch, we decided to go to Holy Island, which was a new experience for me, taking Joey with us. I've never driven across a road that floods with the sea every day. With strict times for going to and fro, we had left it a bit late to go over, so it was just a flying visit as we didn't want to get caught in the return tide.

My nose was twitching; where were we? I could smell the

sea again, but we hadn't stopped yet. I stood up on the seat and stretched. Hang on a minute. I can see the sea to my left and the sea to my right. Were we on a boat? I started to whine and put my paws in the back of Dad's seat. What's happening, Dad?

"It's okay, Joey. We are on a road across the sea, and you can get out soon."

That road seemed to go on forever, and my mind played all sorts of tricks on me. Although this was a shallow area, I had visions of being stuck on the island and unable to return to the motorhome. Sometimes, having a vivid imagination is not good. But we were soon parked up, and we had a chance to have a quick walk around.

Ooh, look, sand...I can do zoomies!

My arm was almost tugged off as Joey suddenly went bonkers. It didn't matter how old this chap got; zoomies were his favourite thing ever. As there were other tourists around, he drew quite an audience, and I just grew giddy, but he was having fun, bouncing around and doing his happy bark. Of course, this followed with lots of cuddles from people who had enjoyed his zoomies and photos being taken of 'such a sweet little boy'.

I was getting twitchy for the tide times. I did not want to cross the road with water lapping at my wheels. Small waves were reaching the edge of the road as we approached. I drove across gingerly, my mind going into overdrive that we would be engulfed in a tidal wave. Breathing a sigh of relief when we made the other side, we pulled over and got out to watch the tide envelop the road like someone doing a zip-up on a jacket. Joey was now not too impressed as his paws were getting wet.

"Come on then, let's get back to the motorhome and get you fed."

Tomorrow, we were hitching the car up and off to Hawick.

Chapter Forty-One

What can I hear now? I knew I was going deaf, but was it a screeching cat? I poked my head up at the window. No, there were no cats, but a lot of men were in skirts. What was going on here then?

We parked up, and I was eager to get out, see what was happening, and see if I could smell cats. I dragged Mom out the door and sniffed. Bugger, no cats. I worked my way around the motorhome to where these men in skirts made cat noises, some of which were hurting my ears. Mom was on the phone, and I heard her say we were in Scotland and were being greeted by bagpipers. Hmmm, these squealing things were bagpipers...basically men in skirts with noisy things. I dragged Mom towards one of them; I needed to sniff. He was a nice man who bent down to give me a fuss.

"Joey, no!"

There was a sharp jerk on my lead. I was only investigating under the man's skirt Mom, honest!

It may seem strange, but we were not on an ordinary

campsite on this occasion but on an aire on the edge of Hawick. Aires are popular on the continent, but very few are in the UK. Hawick was a new area for us to visit, and they have made an area specifically for self-contained motorhomes to park up for the night. This one is free and in a lovely location on the edge of the town.

Hawick is the largest of the Scottish border towns and is famous for its fine-quality knitwear. The town dates back to the 12th century, and many mills were water-powered in the early days. Hawick has been at the fore in many battles, losing most of its menfolk at the Battle of Flodden in 1513. The high street has a mix of modern and old-fashioned shops in historic buildings. Narrow alley-ways intersected the shops, leading to another street or house. Feeling the need for a sit-down, we dropped into a dog-friendly café. There were no more than six small tables inside. I settled Joey whilst David went to order, and I looked up when I heard him laughing. He came to the table, followed by a waitress who immediately knelt to fuss Joey.

"Oh, what a sweet boy. How old is he?"

Here we go again. "He's eighteen."

"No! He looks like a puppy! Hey, Sonia, have you seen this wee boy, he's eighteen."

Joey was in his element as a short queue of customers and staff came over to say hello to him. You really can't take this boy anywhere without him getting attention!

This weekend was the Hawick Reivers Festival, so there were a lot of campers and people coming into town for it. Our neighbours in the car park were the funfair rides and other campers. It's a weekend of 16th-century re-enactments in the town from when the Borderlands were constantly feuding to protect their own. Reiving [to raid and plunder] was a means of survival.

Back at the motorhome, I was outside with Joey when a young girl walked past. Joey's tail was thumping against my leg; he had instantly taken a liking to this young lady. We chatted, and Joey got lots of fuss as she told me she was with the fair and had a Patterdale Terrier. Joey had once more grabbed attention. She came around to see Joey and bring him a treat every day. And every day, Joey knew she was close by as he would either pull at his lead or woof at the door. I'm sure he was quite disappointed when the festival finished, and the fair moved on.

When we left Hawick, we headed back down through Northumberland and stopped over at the back of a pub. Strategic planning so we could eat out rather than cook, and the pub was dog friendly.

Ooh, a pub; I like pubs as I get told I'm an excellent pub dog. I think that has to do with my puppy-dog eyes. We were seated at a table in a quiet area. I quickly sniffed the floor to reveal nothing of interest, then jumped up on the sofa beside Mom before I was turfed off. Hmmph. I lay on the floor with my nose between my paws, watching the door. Then I felt a nip at my tail. I was immediately alert. Wassat?

I jumped to my feet and turned to look.

"Yap, yap," wag.

"Woof."

"Yap, yap," wag.

"Woof, woof."

It was a dachshund, and he wanted to play. For once in my life, I had a playmate that was smaller than me!

I thought it was a rat that scurried behind my legs, but it was a dachshund puppy who had spied Joey. After a quick nip at his tail, he scooted backwards, then came forward again with a yap and a wag of his short tail.

Joey seemed to struggle to make him out for a minute, but then he joined his yapping with a few woofs and went onto all fours in play mode.

The landlord came hurrying around the corner. "Oh, I'm sorry. Is Bertie bothering you?"

"No, it's fine, honest. They seem to be getting on okay."

"Just let me know if he becomes a pain. As pub dogs go, he's a cheeky bugger."

Bertie trotted off after his owner for a minute, and Joey relaxed again. But just as we thought he had gone for good, he returned with a ball. A ball he wasn't going to let go of. He would come in front of Joey and put it down. Then, the minute Joey sniffed it, Bertie grabbed it and scampered under the chairs. Joey had no chance of getting near it as he couldn't follow. The pair kept this up for ages until Bertie's owner brought in our meal, and he was ushered away.

Hmmm. He was a cheeky little chappy, but he was fun. But now Mom and Dad had food, so I was going to be dutiful and lie down to await any falling scraps. In fact, I was dozing off when I heard yap, yap in my ear. What the heck? Bertie was back!

Until I got some titbits, I wasn't playing! Yap, yap, yap!

Bertie was goading me to play. Running up to me, yapping, and then scurrying away under tables and chairs.

Okay, okay, I give in.

I waited for him to come near me again with my eyes half closed. He commando crawled towards me, and just as he was about to yap, I jumped up. Big eyes stared at me in shock as Bertie scrabbled on the tile floor before diving under the chairs. I went to follow but I couldn't get under them. I weaved around the other chairs towards Bertie, who was yapping at the other side of the room. When I got there, he was sitting by Mom and Dad on the sofa. How dare he? I ran over, only for him to dive under the sofa. There was no way I could even attempt to get under there, so I just snuffled under the edge. Then his nose popped out between Dad's legs; he yapped, then dived back under again only to appear by Mom. I was exhausted!

I decided to wave the white flag. Bertie had won, and I wanted my titbits.

Chapter Forty-Two

Once back home, we continued to settle nicely into the community. Joey had many new doggy friends, and his walks were a great way for us to meet new people. We kept friends back in the Midlands updated on social media, and it nearly always featured Joey doing the zoomies. Joey had a knack for making other people happy. Out of the blue, I was contacted by a fellow writer and artist who creates a beautiful newsletter every month. "Would Joey be interested in doing a piece for my newsletter?"

"What do you think, Joey, want to feature in it?"

I assumed the woof of a reply meant yes, so I awaited Alyson to send the questions over, and this is how Joey answered them.

Hello! Can you tell us who you live with?

Woof!

My mom, Alison, and dad, David, live in my new house.

And how did they find you? (Are you a rescue dog, or did they buy you as a puppy?)

When my dad died when I was 10, I was left in some kennels. Then, this lady came along and fussed me. I didn't care much, but she took me for walks. I just wanted my dad. Then I got put in the back of this little white van, and I barked and barked and barked. The lady had taken me to her home. It smelt nice and it was warm, but I wasn't going to let her know that.

Do you have a favourite toy or game?

A toy? I never had toys, so I don't really know what to do with them. Mom gave me some cuddly squeakies, so I tore them to shreds to get the squeaky out! I was very pleased, but Mom was not. She bought me a big yellow duck: I humped that! My favourite thing to do is zoomies on the beach. Even though I'm eighteen, I do great zoomies!

And what are the treats or food you love most?

Meat! I love it when Dad cooks, and I get little bits of meat in my dinner. I also love Schmackos and chicken strips. I've recently become partial to Mom's biscuits that she dunks in her tea!

Do you have any nicknames?

Hmm...I'm deaf now, so I don't answer any of them anymore, but the usual ones are Ratbag and Floofball. Our old neighbour used to call me Shakespeare because of my huge ruff. My dad calls me some really strange names when I get under his feet and trip him up.

What's the naughtiest thing you have ever done?

I have never been naughty, but I am wilful. When Mom first had me, I liked to go my own way and investigate. To do this, I had to escape through doors and dodge the traffic to get to the scent I wanted to sniff or work a hole in the garden hedge to get to the neighbour's garden. I've dived out of the motorhome, too!

Where is the best place for your humans to take you for walkies?

The beach! We are a short drive away from the new house, and I love it. As soon as I get there, I bark and do zoomies. Then I let my nose find the tiny clams and rotting small crabs. If I can get away with it, I crunch them up. Mmmm, I love them.

Are there any tricks or clever things that you can do?

I'm very good at timekeeping. I get Mom up nice and early, and I know exactly when I want my food-the same time every day or earlier if I can get away with it. Mom also bought me a snuffle mat; I'm very good at finding hidden treats.

What's your most favourite thing in the whole world?

Meat, zoomies, and after I've eaten my breakfast, I like to go back to bed with Dad. This may seem lazy, but we are up most mornings before 6 am. That quilt is so soft. Dad is lucky he gets to share it with me!

Where do you sleep at night?

With Mom and Dad on their nice squishy bed. In winter, if Dad is not there, I have been known to sneak under the quilt-purely to keep Mom warm, of course.

Do you have any other animal friends that you play with?

I have made lots of new friends since we moved, but I love it when I see my friend, Nelson. He's very serious and more aloof than me. He tried to sleep in my bed once, which was funny, as he is three times my size!

And if you give the world one piece of advice, what would it be?

Learn to do puppy eyes at humans; you will get anything you want.

[www.alysonsheldrake.com/snapshot-archive]

Questions were completed, and photos were sent. We awaited publication the following month. It was great to see our boy featured in such a great newsletter! We shared it with everyone we knew! One friend came back with this comment: "Very kind of you to let your mummy tag stuff about her at the end of the article. When is Joey the movie coming out?"

I don't think he needs any encouragement. Thank you, Alan!

Chapter Forty-Three

Once we had settled in our new home, David's daughter, Helen, visited with her dog Amber. Amber is a very cute Pomchi [Pomeranian/Chihuahua cross.]

Ooh, who is this?

I stood at the side gate, and Mom and Dad were chatting with a lady outside. I woofed. The lady reached into the car, and out came this little poofy thing. It was small even to me!

The lady was Helen. Hmm, okay, but who was this little pooch?

"Joey, this is Amber."

My lead was put on, and Amber was coming in through the gate on her lead with Helen. For once, I didn't have to look up at another dog; I could stand and look down!

We sniffed a bit, and then Amber gave me a snooty look and promptly lost interest. Oh, that's okay then. I think!

Dad released my lead, and Helen let Amber off, too.

I blinked. Amber wandered off, totally ignoring me! I

followed her as she sniffed around the garden. Wherever she had a wee, I followed suit.

Mom, Dad and Helen were watching us. What for guys, we are just doing dog things?

"Come on, guys, inside!"

Both of us took little notice until I saw the treat bag. Oh, yeah, that'll do for me.

We both trotted obediently into the house and followed Mom, who had the treats. We both sat: the picture of obedience. Mom handed us each a treat.

Realising there were no more in the offing, I decided to sniff at Amber again. Oops, that didn't go down too well, she snapped at me before jumping onto the footstool. I tried to get up, too, but she growled. Hmmph, sod you then, I'll lie on my bed, at which point Amber got down and came and laid on the edge of my bed with a flounce! I ignored her. If she wanted to play hard to get, then turn on the charm to get my cosy spot, it wasn't going to happen.

After a few minutes, I dozed off, but I was quickly awoken when I heard Helen say, Oh Amber!

I opened one eye to see half a dozen blobs the size of Maltesers on the carpet. Amber had disgraced herself. If dogs could laugh, I would have, but I decided better of it and remained half asleep.

"Amber's a little cow for doing that in other people's houses," said Helen as she quickly scooped up Amber's poops in a little bag, "I'm really sorry."

"Oh, don't worry, it could have been worse."

After that, the dogs settled in perfect ignorance of each other.

The following day, we went to Joey's favourite place, the beach. He was in his element as ever, zooming around and making me giddy. Amber just trotted off to do her own thing. They remained aloof from each other, but at least they weren't arguing!

When Helen and Amber left, Joey was certainly non-plussed. I think he thought she was a bossy-boots.

Chapter Forty-Four

We discovered new places to go in the motorhome, which also meant new friends for Joey. One camping site just ten miles away became a favourite, and Joey loved going into the woods there. From there, we could go into Brigg for market day. Brigg is a lovely old market town with a lovely mix of fresh vegetables, meat, and fish stalls. Our favourite was a locally made cheese stall. We liked to try a new cheese each time we went, often buying two or three to gorge on for supper with crackers and pickles.

We were walking by some local craft stalls, and there was an elderly lady in a wheelchair enjoying looking at the home-crafted items. Her carer was also chatting with her and the stall holder. We were about to walk by when she caught sight of me. Of course, I wagged my tail and went towards her.

"Oh, you sweet little dog, can I stroke you?"

She put her hand down towards me but couldn't quite reach me. Mom scooped me up so that the lady could see me.

Her face was super smiley. The stall holder and her carer were forgotten as the slightly shaking, wizened hand approached me. I stayed very still and quiet as she caressed my fur and stroked my ears. There were tears in her eyes as she enjoyed the moment she was enveloped in, nothing else in the world existed at that moment in time.

"Oh, you are such a sweet little boy. I used to have a little dog who loved to sleep on my lap; I'm sure you like to do that too, don't you?"

I was enjoying all this attention, and everyone else had stopped talking and was watching me and the lady enjoying the moment.

I was getting heavy in Mom's arms, and she had to put me down.

"Thank you, young man, for making my day." *Then she blew me a kiss.*

Mom was praising me as we walked away. It was great, so I wagged my tail and barked with joy.

David and I said our goodbyes, and we walked on, neither of us saying anything for a few minutes. I had tears in my eyes at the pleasure Joey had brought that lady. It was an extraordinary moment for all of us. I could imagine the conversation on her way back to her care home and the tales she would tell when she returned.

Chapter Forty-Five

We had noticed for some time that Joey was not answering to his name when called and had assumed he was going deaf. The vet agreed with us, so a plan of action was called for, hand signals. Okay, it was not always easy when he wasn't looking at you, but by and large, it worked. Plus, his nose went into sensory overdrive. Any time David was cooking, Joey was there like a shot. He wound himself in between his legs, much like a cat does.

This caused David no end of problems, as he has a dodgy knee. The call of "Oh, Joey!" from the kitchen occasionally came with a bang or a crash, as David managed to avoid falling flat on his face when Joey got right in the way. Joey just wagged his tail. You couldn't be angry at the boy even when he was a nuisance.

I always got Joey trimmed before the summer, but that had gone by the wayside with all the moving going on, and he was getting desperate. Being a cocker and sheltie blend, there was a lot of floof! He had loved his previous groomer, Lisa, and was spoiled rotten there, but now we had moved, we had to find a new one.

We were recommended one called A Classic Clip on the Grimsby/Cleethorpes border, so we went to meet Jess. It was love at first sight for both of them. We explained that Joey was old and deaf, and she assured us that she would keep in contact with him as she groomed him so that he felt secure. I always hate leaving dogs at the groomers: I'm sure it stresses me more than them! I constantly look at my phone and expect the worst, that he has been naughty or something equally silly.

We left him there and went to the supermarket nearby to stock up on some essentials before heading to Riby Street and the fishmongers. We had been lucky to discover Riby Street from, once more, the locals in the village. The fishmongers always used to be in Grimsby Docks but had moved out over time and were mostly situated in this area now. It was at the back of the docks, so the catch didn't have to travel far to the wholesalers and retailers. We walked into Premier Seafoods and were struck by an array of wonderful goodies.

It was the grown-up version of being a child and going into the local sweetshop where you had to be on tiptoes to peer at the trays of brightly coloured sweets, all ready for you to choose a penny mix from. There was so much choice of fish and shellfish, smoked and unsmoked, that it was hard to choose what to have. Of course, the main fish in the area was haddock, and my word, the haddock here was huge, relatively cheap, and super fresh: from trawler to slab. It hadn't even travelled half a mile.

David was struck dumb. "There's too much choice," he said. "Can we just have a minute to browse?"

Julie smiled. "You carry on; let me know when you're ready."

I knew exactly what David meant. There were scallops, mussels, whelks, clams, razor clams and prawns so big that one was a meal on its own. Sea bass, monkfish, haddock, cod, whiting, eel, and more. It wasn't easy to choose what fresh fish to have before you got to the frozen section that had massive fish fingers that were made of beautiful cod fillets that flaked away, Whitby scampi: the best scampi you can get, squid rings and mixed seafood that was great for paella. I was used to Birmingham Fish Market when we lived in the Midlands, but this was something else.

I felt my phone buzz in my pocket as I chose some haddock and seabass fillets. 'Joey is ready.' We quickly paid and headed back to pick up the boy.

We opened the door to a very sheepish-looking bundle of shorter-coated Joey. Jess stood there with him in her arms, and he was loving every minute of his cuddles!

"Oh, he has been so good!"

"No nipping or anything?" I was surprised.

"No, not a thing. I just kept him close. No problem being bathed either."

"He's had a bath?"

"Oh yes, he loved it!"

"Jess, he rarely has a bath; he hates them! I'm flabbergasted. You little devil, Joey!" I laughed.

I was sad to leave Jess; she had spoiled me rotten, and I'd had lots of cuddles, but I wasn't going to tell Mom and Dad that. I got into the car and was clipped into the harness and seatbelt. I did my usual barking before settling. I was glad to be back with Mom and Dad, and I didn't smell too sweet and girly either! There was no need for me to scrub along the furniture when I got home to get my doggy smell back. With all my long floof cut off, I felt much cooler and bouncier. I now needed zoomies as I felt so fresh and light with my new haircut!

Chapter Forty-Six

We had been in the new house for over a year, and it had gone by quickly. We were both involved with the village hall and the community in general. Life was good, and having the whole of Lincolnshire and Yorkshire to explore in our motorhome was great.

Joey, however, was starting to show his age. We had him on a supplement that helped with his stiff back legs and allowed him to keep doing his zoomies. This totally amazed the new vet when we went in for our first visit. With his hands giving Joey a thorough check-over, he said, "His heart is in good shape; how is he doing in himself?"

"Well, he's deaf and has slowed down a little, but otherwise he's okay."

"Oh, and he still does zoomies," said David.

The vet gave us a quizzical look. "He does zoomies at eighteen?"

"Oh, yes, he will do them when we return home."

The vet looked at me as if I was delusional.

"Let me show you."

I pulled out my phone and started flicking through the videos. "Here you go; this was last week."

Volume up, I played a forty-second video of Joey doing what he does best, bouncing around the garden like a puppy.

The vet smiled, "That is remarkable for a dog his age; he looks so happy."

With that, we departed the vets with a happy dog and left an amazed vet behind.

Joey started waking up in the middle of the night and wanting to go out. Then he began to have what we thought was an upset tummy, and we would wake up to find him desperate to go out but never really doing anything when he got there.

After a few days, I called the vet and arranged an appointment. I explained how he had been over the previous months and that, in general, he seemed fine, but his body clock was well out of sync. A diet of rice and chicken was advised, and treatment for a tummy bug was administered, and we left with the hope that all would be well. But inside, I had a sinking feeling that it wouldn't be.

After a few months of this new pattern of midnight garden visits, I was exhausted and often had a doze in the afternoon to compensate for the broken sleep and the worry. Joey snuggled up next to me and dozed, too. As a nineteen-year-old dog, he had lived a wonderful life, and I often cried myself to sleep at night at the thought of losing him. I really couldn't imagine life without him by my side.

For now, I convinced myself it was his age and that life was as it would be for the foreseeable future.

A few weeks later, a friend asked about the lump that had developed on Joey's jaw just beneath his left eye. I had assumed it was a cyst, but I also noticed it was getting bigger. As he still wasn't right in himself, I arranged another visit to the vet. I think this was just a sign of him getting older because he seemed so normal in many ways. Well, at one hundred and thirty-three in doggy years, he was pretty old!

Another trip to the vet was nerve-jangling. I once more explained that he wasn't himself and was worried about the lump. After a careful and caring examination, she gave us the worst news. It was cancer and, with the strange behaviour, the start of doggy dementia. As Joey was fine in himself and didn't appear to be in pain, we went home via a trip to the beach. A good dose of fresh air and Joey zoomies were what we needed, and it did us all good.

It was a subdued evening at home. All I wanted to do was cuddle my little boy, knowing we were on borrowed time, but Joey wasn't sinking into my arms like he normally would. He seemed to sit there looking lost. David, like me, was lost in his world, too. This boy was precious to both of us.

"Let's go out in the van."

David booked a local site, and two days later, we went to Withern Mill Trout Farm for a week.

Withern Mill is a lovely little site with just five pitches. Quiet and down a dead-end lane: we loved it there. It was a trout breeding farm that supplied the trade in Grimsby and further afield. It also allowed fishermen to fish in its many lakes. The rolling fields around it made for beautiful sunsets, too. It was time to relax and enjoy the day.

Joey was now not eating very much, and we had him on an almost permanent diet of rice, chicken, and fish. I was pretty much always sleeping on the bench seat of the motorhome so I could be there for him if he needed me. When he woke me in the night, I popped on my head torch and grabbed a handful of poo bags before going outside to walk around in circles until Joey managed to do his business. It is heartbreaking knowing you can't do anything for them other than be there.

After another few days, I broke down in tears.

"I can't do this anymore, David. He has no quality of life, and it's getting worse every day."

I sobbed as my heart broke into little pieces. The three of us sat there cuddling.

I'm tired now, Mom; I need to go to sleep.

"I'm going to call the vets in the morning. It's just not fair on him anymore."

The trip to the vet was harrowing. How I held myself together, I don't know. David had tears streaming down his face as I stroked and talked to Joey in his final moments. It was a harrowing experience, but I knew I had to be strong for him. The vet left us to be with him for as long as we wished. It was the hardest thing to do: turning our backs on our boy and leaving through the waiting area of other owners and pets awaiting treatment. But it was all a blur.

With lead and collar in our pockets, we headed back to the motorhome, where we both cried our eyes out. That wonderful boy had been in my life for nine of his nineteen years. He had been my saviour at a time when I needed him, and he was going to leave a massive hole in our lives.

Chapter Forty-Seven

Back home, we both dreaded walking into the house. It was all so quiet. No Joey doing zoomies in the garden, barking with joy. We hung his lead in the usual place and popped his collar on the mantlepiece. His empty bed was in the lounge, and bits of floof were on the carpet. But our boy was at peace and had had a good life; no, he had had a great life. I vowed not to dwell on his demise but to celebrate his life: that was more important.

I decided to let everyone know straight away. So many people loved Joey, and I felt they needed to know what had happened. We had not mentioned him being poorly to anyone: it was a private time, so it all came as a shock to everyone. On social media, I posted a video of the zoomies that Joey had done just two weeks before and broke the news. I wasn't expecting the reaction we received. So much empathy and tears from those who had never met Joey or us. So many messages said they looked forward to his videos, and it always cheered them up and made them happy. I always thought Joey was on this earth to bring joy and happiness, and I was sure he had achieved that.

The following weeks alternated between normality and sorrow. I would go out in the garden, and in my mind, I could see Joey pottering and sniffing or zooming from the side gate to the back hedge, head held high, giving happy barks. I often talked to him when I was out there. Nothing earth-shattering, just the everyday things that would have been said had he been there. Late at night, when it was quiet, I felt solace in the darkness as the tears flowed down my cheeks.

I had yet to break the news to Joey's friends in the village, so I began walking to the shop at the normal walk time to hopefully bump into some of them. In a small village like ours, I knew that they would let the rest know once I'd told a couple of people. It was also a good excuse to get some doggy cuddles, as I was missing the comfort of my little furry buddy.

The first few times I had to say that Joey had died out loud were horrendous. It was bad enough on social media to explain what had happened to those who asked, but saying it out loud was excruciating.

A few weeks later, I received a surprise email from Alyson Sheldrake, who had previously interviewed Joey for her newsletter. Would I mind if she included a memorial piece on Joey in her next issue? Well, of course not! I wanted to celebrate his life, and what could be better?

Here is what she wrote.

"We were desperately saddened to learn that Joey Moore had passed away last month. He was the first dog that Kat interviewed in her new Kat's Kuestions feature, and his answers were a delight. He was a much-loved senior dog who will be missed so much; our hearts go out to Alison and her family at this sad time. The pain we felt losing Kat is something we will never truly get over, and we will always miss her and never forget her. We hope in time, they, too, will be able to remember with fondness the good times with Joey and how special he was.

We had planned to share this poem below with you all this month, but it seems even more appropriate now."

A Letter from the Rainbow Bridge

Hi, Mom and Dad!

Now that I've been across The Rainbow Bridge for a couple of weeks, they said I should write a letter home. Sorry, Mom, but I'm so busy 'across the bridge' that I haven't thought of home much. They said it was okay and that you would understand. I hope you do. (I think you will.)

Remember that night when I wasn't feeling very well, and we were all crying? I don't remember much, but I do remember seeing and hearing all of you and feeling your touches and hugs...I remember hearing "We love you" and that one last command of "Go through". I didn't know what you meant, so I turned around and walked through the fog that was in front of me. I saw the biggest bridge I've ever seen! And so many friends on the other side of it! They were all playing with toys and balls! You were right to tell me to go there!

My feet kept moving forward, but my heart kept pulling me back. Your touches became lighter and lighter and I wanted to come back and nudge your hands for more love, but I was overcome by this feeling of curiosity for the happy place over the bridge! My feet started moving on their own, like a gentle breeze was moving them forward for me! I can't explain it, but I had no doubt that it was the right thing to do!

So, I walked across that big, huge bridge by myself! I looked for you because you're always by my side, walking with me, but this was different. I didn't have a collar around my neck or a leash connecting me to you-I was 'free'! Even though you weren't there with me, I never felt alone! I actually felt like I had a huge cape of love wrapped around my body and the more I walked, the easier it was to breathe! So, I kept walking! And I would feel more warmth in the big hug, so I kept on walking! I eventually made it over the big bridge-I did it by myself, Mom!

When I got here, all of my new friends greeted me and helped me walk off the bridge-it was so cool! They gave me a pair of wings and said that I was now a Guardian Angel!

What I've learned over these past few weeks has been amazing and nothing like I've seen before! We're all the same up here-we all have wings and we all have Forever People to watch over-that's YOU, Mom! You're my Forever Person, and I'm your Forever Pet. We had such a great life together and I do miss you a LOT, but please know that I am so happy in my new home across The Bridge!

I'll send you another Earth Angel so you won't be alone. Give them your whole heart like you gave it to me. I'll check in every so often to ensure they treasure your love-I always did! When you miss me, think of a rainbow and know I'm on the other side of it, waiting to walk with you again. I'll always be in your heart. I love you, Mom and Dad! Time for me to go play...."

By Donna Erickson

Chapter Forty-Eight

AFTER JOEY

The photo I have used of Joey on the cover is one of my favourites. David took it not long after he had moved in and it shows him at his finest.

I have always wanted to draw Joey, but I have always put commissions of other dog portraits first. Now, I can't do it. Maybe in time, but not yet.

One of the Facebook groups I belonged to was for artist reference photos. I decided to put Joey's picture there if anyone was interested in drawing or painting him. With over ninety-two thousand members, I figured someone might want a black-and-white fluffy dog to work on. Once more, I was astounded by the response. Over the following months, fourteen people posted various paintings, drawings, and depictions of Joey, inspired by his handsome good looks and my story of losing him.

Three extraordinary people insisted on sending me their artwork as a memento of my beautiful boy. They were sent to me from various points around the globe, and they now surround us every day.

When we were at the vet for that final visit, they kindly and gently snipped off some of his fur for us to keep: black, white, and grey strands. I wasn't sure what I would do with them, but I knew it was a small memento I wanted to have.

Some were secured on the back of the needle-felted picture, and other strands I popped into keychains with a picture of Joey that I had sketched several years ago. These were going to be given to the few special people who I knew were missing Joey the most and who he loved dearly.

The days were quiet. Joey's bed in the lounge and the one in the bedroom sat unused. We couldn't bear to remove either of them.

There was no happy barking and zoomies.

Gone were the early starts to the day and the nagging for breakfast and dinner.

Gone were David's shouts when he was cooking. These were the moments when Joey would place himself right underneath him to catch any titbits dropped, managing to easily trip David up.

Gone were the scraping paws as he tried to reach his after-dinner treats, which waited on the work surface.

There were so many little things that we missed.

Those pleading eyes after a steak titbit, pinching your chair when you got up, including my camping chair. Him sleeping on my lap or leaning up on me on the bed and, of course, the zoomies.

It made me happy to share his photos and zoomie

videos on Facebook; so many people had gotten to know Joey from my Facebook feed and his own page. I received so many empathetic messages that it was humbling. Joey had had such a happy impact on people's lives worldwide: we weren't the only ones who would miss him dearly.

I was already partway through writing another book, but I decided to put that aside and continue with this one. I started it many years ago, but like many things, work and life got in the way of continuing. Completing it felt like an essential part of my healing.

We also knew Joey would want us to adopt another rescue dog, but were we ready?

We began following many rescue centres on Facebook and looking on the internet, too. We didn't mind what we adopted; we knew we could give a dog or a pair of dogs a good, loving home.

Nina and Simone appeared on the computer screen, and they were gorgeous Cocker Spaniel ladies who had been used for breeding. David filled in the paperwork, and we were called quickly to see them. They were beautiful and very friendly.

These gorgeous ladies bounded towards us with tails wagging, expecting a fuss and a cuddle. We walked them around the paddock, each showing her personality by lunging ahead or trailing behind. They were just beautiful.

The rescue centre had a house where you could go with the dogs to see how they interacted indoors. Nina and Simone happily plodded about the place before going into the back garden, but then they came indoors for a wee. Ah, toilet training would be an issue, then. We called them to us in the garden and tried to encourage them to play with toys, sadly without success. It was sad that they did not know their names at five and six years old and had never been house-trained or knew how to play with toys.

After such a lovely meeting, we left to think it over, and I promptly retreated into my shell. We had decided to discuss it when we got home. That journey was agony. I didn't know what David was thinking and vice versa. I was totally confused because, in reality, I only wanted Joey. Once home, I realised I couldn't do it. I wasn't ready.

I burst into tears and sobbed myself to sleep in the chair. Although I felt the time wasn't right, it did me good to release the emotion. I could still see the mix of images of Joey doing zoomies and the last visit to the vet: a moment I wanted to forget even though it was peaceful and calm.

I switched off all notifications for dog rescues for a month and tried to put it to the back of my mind. I knew I needed to heal and regain my energy before taking on another dog. It wasn't fair to a new rescue dog for me not to be 100%.

The pain was easing a little after a few weeks of getting my sleep pattern back and feeling more on top of things. Every time I went out in the back garden, I could still see Joey bounding around, but it was a sweet memory. The devil on my shoulder was always asking the same question: had I done right by him? The logical answer is yes; he had cancer and dementia near the end, and he was no longer living his best life. The cancer was getting him fast, and it wasn't fair to keep him going for our own sake.

I concentrated on starting to read what I had already written about him and began making notes: I focussed on his memory, and that made me smile. Because I managed to talk about him, people spoke to me about him too. It was a great healing process.

In writing breaks, I dipped into a rescue site or two. The number of dogs needing a home was overwhelming. David loved all and every dog! I was a tad more realistic about what suited us best. We flitted from standard poodles to dachshunds and everything in between. Neither of us will go for two-mile walks daily for something big and lively. Plus, there were breed mixes that were, on personal preference, ones we didn't like. I feel guilty saying that, but we all have our favourites.

I will say now that I love mixed breeds, cockers, dachshunds, and schnauzers, but I am not limiting my search. Let's see where we end up!

We were realistic about the distance from animal rescue centres, too. Who knew there were so many around the country? A cocker rescue centre in South Wales had a dozen or more they had just rescued, but the five-hour drive there was crazy. It's so sad; so many dogs need homes. Unfortunately, some rescue centres wanted money up front to bring a dog in from abroad, which was a big gamble on the dog's getting here and us not knowing its temperament. We were surprised that some centres even wanted to choose the dog that they deemed suitable for you: that wasn't going to happen.

Then, this little face cropped up at one rescue centre that was local to us: he was called Smudge. Once more,

David filled in the forms and sent them off. And we waited. A few days later, he had a message saying the foster carer would contact us. We sent the obligatory videos of the home and garden to show it was secure and waited.

Two days later, we had a long phone call with the foster mom. He sounded perfect, so a visit to the rescue centre was arranged.

Off we went, already feeling that this was the boy for us. I felt really positive this time, unlike with the cockers, where I just wanted to get out of there in a blind panic. As we went through the gate, we saw this bundle of black fur leaping around the conservatory, barking his head off: it was Smudge.

He came out on his lead, gave us a look and a wag, and headed for the garden area. He was funny-looking but cute. If you imagine a black border collie with corgi legs, you have Smudge. He seemed calm and rolled over for a belly rub before wandering off for a good sniff. Well, we impressed him then!

Smudge will come to live with us in two weeks. This is only because we booked a holiday and felt it wasn't fair for him to be messed around so quickly, and the rescue centre agreed. His new cage and bed are in place, and we bought some toys for him. Joey will live on happily in our memories, but now it's time to give Smudge a taste of the good life. Joey did indeed send us our Earth Angel.

Other books by Alison J Moore

If you have enjoyed this book, please leave a review on Amazon.
Thank You.

You can catch up on Joey's exploits and what we learn about Smudge on their very own Facebook page, called **Joey and Smudge. https://www.facebook.com/utterlycutedog/**

All About Dog

As many people know, adopting a rescue dog is hard work. You can train a puppy as you go along, but a rescue is pretty much set in its ways.

Joey was a rescue, and I knew nothing about his previous life. This time, I wanted to learn as much as I could. I started writing questions that would be important for both us and the dog to settle in with each other. When we got Smudge home, this proved invaluable, so I turned it into a book.

Now, Smudge's personality traits, habits and everything else are recorded in one place forever.

Calamity Camping

'Have toilets really changed so much over the years that I have been going camping?'

Join Alison in this humorous collection of memories from over

50 years of camping whether it be in a tent, caravan or motorhome.

Toilets seem to crop up with frequency along with beautiful locations and the idiosyncrasies of the outdoor life.

Calamity Spain

The first time I got onto a plane on my own set me off on a new path in life without realising it. A new path to freedom, exploring places I would never have gone to had I still been part of a couple. To making friends who lived in another country and wanting to live where the sun shone and life was at a slower, healthier pace.

I wanted to have my own little slice of a Spanish village and live the life that it offered. I was going to fulfil my dream to buy a place abroad in the Sierra Nevada and live happily ever after. I knew where I wanted to be I now just had to make it happen. Little did I know the roller coaster journey I would have.

Find out what's new by going to

www.alisonjmoore.com

Printed in Great Britain
by Amazon

61356588R00147